SHOULDA BEEN JIMI SAVANNAH

Shoulda Been Jimi Savannah

POEMS

Patricia Smith

COFFEE HOUSE PRESS

Minneapolis

COFFEE HOUSE PRESS books are available to the trade through our primary distributor, Consortium Book Sales & Distribution, www.cbsd.com. For personal orders, catalogs, or other information, write to: Coffee House Press, 79 Thirteenth Avenue NE, Suite 110, Minneapolis, MN 55413.

Coffee House Press is a nonprofit literary publishing house. Support from private foundations, corporate giving programs, government programs, and generous individuals helps make the publication of our books possible. We gratefully acknowledge their support in detail in the back of this book. To you and our many readers around the world, we send our thanks for your continuing support.

Good books are brewing at coffeehousepress.org

LIBRARY OF CONGRESS CIP INFORMATION
Smith, Patricia, 1955–
Shoulda been Jimi Savannah / Patricia Smith.
p. cm.
ISBN 978-1-56689-299-5 (alk. paper)
I. Title.
PS3569.M537839S56 2012
811'.54—DC22
2011029282

1 3 5 7 9 8 6 4 2

PRINTED IN CANADA
FIRST EDITION | FIRST PRINTING

ACKNOWLEDGMENTS
The author wishes to thank the editors of the following publications where these works first appeared: *Asheville Poetry Review:* "Still Life with Toothpick," "Before Orphan Unearthed the Mirror"; *Best American Essays 2011:* "Pearl, Upward," (comprised of the poems "How a Mama Begins Sometimes," "Annie Pearl, Upward" and "June 25, 1955"); *Best American Poetry 2011:* "Motown Crown"; *Bop, Strut, and Dance: A Post-Blues Form for New Generations:* "Annie Pearl's ArethaBops"; *Chautauqua Literary Journal:* "Thief of Tongues"; *City of Big Shoulders—An Anthology of Chicago Poetry:* "Chicago"; *Crab Orchard Review:* "Pearl, Upward"; *Cutthroat:* "Carnie," "Next. Next." "Shedding"; *Gargoyle:* "Because," "Dear Jimmy Connoll"; *Granta:* "A Colored Girl Will Slice You If You Talk Wrong about Motown"; *Killer Verse—Poems of Mayhem and Murder:* "Speculation"; *PMS— Poem/Memoir/Story:* "An All-Purpose Product"; *Poetry:* "Hip-Hop Ghazal"; *Rattle:* "Tavern. Tavern. Tavern. Shuttered tavern," "Motown Crown"; *Reverie—Midwest African-American Literature:* "Doubledutch," "Closest to Heaven"; *River Styx:* "Tenzone," "Ooo, Baby, Baby"; *Roanoke Review:* "His for the Taking"; *Sugar House Review:* "First Friction," "Laugh Your Troubles Away!"; *Tin House:* "Baby of the Mistaken Hue"; *Word Warriors— 35 Women Leaders in the Spoken Word Revolution:* "Asking for a Heart Attack."

Special thanks to Kwame Dawes, Cave Canem, the National Book Foundation, and the enduring light of Gwendolyn Brooks. She taught me Chicago.

For all the families that have understood,
nurtured, and sustained me.

And for Bruce and Mikaila, always.

1. OLD BACKDROPS DARK

2. WE SHINED LIKE THE NEW THINGS WE WERE

3. LEARNING TO SUBTRACT

4. MAD AT MY WHOLE DAMN FACE

5. WAIT

He said true things, but called them by wrong names.

—ELIZABETH BARRETT BROWNING

1

OLD BACKDROPS DARK

HOW MAMAS BEGIN SOMETIMES

For my mother, Annie Pearl Smith

determination

Raging tomgirl, blood dirt streaking her thick ankles
and <u>bare feet</u>, she is always running, screech raucous,
careening, dare and games in her clothesline throat.
Playing like she has to play to live, she shoves at what
slows her, steamrolls whatever damn thing won't move.
Aliceville, Alabama's no fool. It won't get in her way.

fighting for the
tomgirl in her

<u>Where's that girl going?</u> Past slant sag porches, pea shuck,
twangy box guitars begging under purple dayfall. Combs
spitting sparks, hair parted and scalps scratched, <u>mules</u>
<u>trembling the back road,</u> the marbled stares of elders
fixed on checkerboards. Cursed futures crammed into
cotton pouches with pinches of bitterroot, the horrid parts
of meat stewed <u>sweet and possible.</u> And still, whispers
about the disappeared, whole <u>souls</u> lost in the passage.

old south /
norm for
her town

gossips of
the ppl of the
old south

we
now
ow they disappeared?   mystical

Frolicking blindly, flailing tough with cousins, sisters,
but running blaze, running on purpose, bounding toward
away. She can't tag this <u>fever,</u> but she believes it knows
her, owns her in a way religion should. Toes tap, feet
flatten out inside the <u>sin of shoes.</u> She is most times
asking something, steady asking, needing to know,
needing to know *now,* taking wing on that blue restless
that drums her. Twisting on rusty hinge, that old porch door
whines for <u>one long second</u> 'bout where she was.

tting on
oes
s again
her
ligion
playing

the
passion of
her play
(HOW religion is
a part of her)

relates to
whispers

But that girl gone.

looking for her,
but she was gone

he was gone
so quickly—
did anyone
really care?

or grown up?

I

STILL LIFE WITH TOOTHPICK

For my father, Otis Douglas Smith,
and the grandparents I never knew

Maybe his father grunted, brusque and focused as he
brawled with the steering, maybe there was enough time
for a flashed invective, some hot-patched dalliance with God.
Then the Plymouth, sounding like a cheated-on woman,
screamed into hurtled revolt and cracked against a tree.

Bone rammed through shoulder, functions imploded,
compounded pulse spat slow thread into the road.
His small stuttering mother's body braided up sloppy
with foliage and windshield, his daddy became
the noon's smeared smile. For hours, they simply rained.

It is Arkansas, so the sky was a cerulean stretch, the sun
a patient wound. The boxy sedan smoldered and spat
along the blistered curve while hounds and the skittering
sniffed the lumping red river and blood birds sliced lazy over
the wreck, patiently waiting for the feast to cool. The sheriff

sidled up, finally, rolled a toothpick across his bottom teeth,
weighed his options. It was 'round lunchtime, the meatloaf
on special, that slinky waitress on call. He climbed
back into his cruiser and drove off, his mind clear. *Awfully nice*
of those poor nigras to help out. Damned if they didn't
just drip right into the dirt. Pretty much buried themselves.

KEEP SAYING HEAVEN AND IT WILL

Otis is orphan in a very slow way. Relatives orbit the folded him, paint his parents to breath with stories that take the long way around trees, stories about the time before the two of them set out in the rumbling Plymouth, going somewhere, not getting there.

Otis is orphan in a very one way. Only one him. Only the solo with only happy stories to hear, no one says *car*. No one says *crash* or *never* or *dead now*. Everyone says *heaven*. They pat his head with flat hands, say *heaven* with all their teeth, say *heaven* with their shredding silk throats. They say *heaven heaven heaven* while their eyes rip days down.

Otis is orphan in a very wide way. They feed him dripping knots of fatback, bowlfuls of peppered collards, cheap chicken pieces sizzled thick and doughy, stewed shards of swine. They dip bread in bowls of melted butter, fry everything, okra and tomatoes, fish skin, gizzards, feet. And the women shovel sugar and coconut meat into baking pans, slosh sweet cream into bowls and stir and bake and it is all everything for him for his little empty gut. They feed him enough for two other people, though no one says *two other people*.

Finally someone says *bodies*. Something about the souls having left them and thank God for that. Someone says *maybe just one casket*. He is eating peaches drifting in a syrup. They think he is a little boy too overloved to hear. But he knows days. And this new sound, *orphan*, which means that mama and daddy are too close to be pulled apart. They are in one pretty place. But only one him, too adored and fattened. There will be a home for them to come back to. He is widening, practicing with his arms. He will be their first warm wall.

BEFORE ORPHAN UNEARTHED THE MIRROR

He was
always told that he looked like everyone, everything—
his mama's brother and sister, that loopy
cockeyed chicken, that droop-tittied store girl.
Nosy folks even said he resembled Earl Lee's
circling mule, or that crumpled picture of Jesus
stapled to the kitchen. When you are not in
the way that he was not, no one admits a root.
Everyone had a hand or paw on him, steady
testifying to the miracle of his standing,
his dogged insistence upon breath. So one
morning he just up and said good-bye.
He swept his eyes slow over the spider
cracks swallowing the crop, the toppled milk
cans and slivered barn roof, his uncle's flat
face, the pummeled tops of his own shoes.
He said good-bye to a shred of his father
folded into the trilling heart of a tree. *I'm
leaving for Chicago* he told his aunt and uncle
and they didn't even try hiding their hallelujah.
All his nose, hands, and stride ever did were
remind them of dead. They hated telling him
how he looked like anything else, everything
else. They were tired of pretending that his face,
scratched and black, wasn't a record that just
kept on skipping, playing that, that song.

some disaster happened—
scars on his face
remind his family of it
and he doesn't remember

FIXING ON THE NEXT STAR

Between 1916 and 1970, more than half a million African-Americans
left the South and migrated to Chicago.

Mamas go quietly crazy, dizzied by the possibilities
of a kitchen, patiently plucking hairs from the skin
of supper. Swinging children from thick forearms,
they hum stanzas riddled with Alabama hue and promises
Jesus may have made. Homes swerve on foundations
while, inside, the women wash stems and shreds of syrup
from their palms and practice contented smiles,
remembering that it's a sin to damn this ritual or foul
the heat-sparkled air with any language less than prayer.

And they wait for their loves, men of marbled shoulders
and exploded nails, their faces grizzled landscapes
of scar and descent. These men stain every room
they enter, drag with them a stench of souring iron.
The dulled wives narrow their eyes, busy themselves
with clanging and stir, then feed the sweating
soldiers whole feasts built upon okra and the peppered
necks of chickens. After the steam dies, chewing
is all there is—the slurp of spiced oil, the crunch
of bone, suck of marrow. And then the conversation,
which never changes, even over the children's squeals:
They say it's better up there, it begins, and it is always
the woman who says this, and the man lowers his head
to the table and feels the day collapse beneath his shirt.

ONE WAY TO RUN FROM IT

The damned boll weevil hisses his good-bye
while cypresses drip low in steamed salute
and satchel-toting travelers multiply,

affixed to that bright dream—the absolute
reversal of their root. Their gospel hum
dissuades the Delta dog, his resolute

pursuit of traitors' souls. The city's drum,
the new unyielding, slaps old backdrops dark.
Chicago, frigid siren, murmurs *Come*

while hiding how she fails—December's stark
and violent entry into bone, the ways
a factory's drone can siphon every spark

of will. She boldly lures them with clichés:
the gilded path, the blur of black and white.
Seduced, they set their Southern pasts ablaze.

Intent on fresh religions, taking flight
without their wings, they're stunned in hurtling seats.
This train moans in a way that ain't quite right.

ANNIE PEARL, UPWARD

Chicago. She's heard the craving out loud, the tales of where money runs like water and after you arrive it takes—*what, a minute?*—to forget that Alabama ever held sweet for you.

She wants to find a factory that works ritual into her knuckles. She's never heard a siren razor the dark. She wants Lucky Strikes, a dose of high life every Friday, hard lessons from a jukebox. Wants to wave bye to her mama. All she needs is a bus ticket, a brown riveted case to hold her gray dress, and a waxed bag crammed with smashed slices of white bread and fat fried slabs of perch. With the whole of her chest, she knows what she's been running toward.

Apple cheek and glory gap-tooth fills the window of the Greyhound. For the upcoming, she has hot-combed her hair into shiver strings and donned a fresh-stitched skirt that wrestles with her curves. This deception is what the city asks. Her head is full and hurting with future until the bus arrives. She stumbles forth with all she owns, wanting to be romanced by some sudden thunder. She tries not to see the brown folks— the whipcloth shoe shiners, the bag carriers—staring at her, searching for some sign, aching for a smell of where she came from.

How does a city sway when you've never seen it before? It's months before she realizes that no one knows her name. No one says *Annie Pearl* and means it.

She crafts a life that is dimmer than she'd hoped, in a tenement with walls pressing in hard and fat roaches, sluggish with Raid, dropping into her food, writhing on the mattress of her Murphy bed. In daytime, she works in a straight line with other women, her hands moving without her. Repeat. Repeat. When her evenings are breezy and free and there is jiggling in her purse, she looks for music that hurts, cool slips of men in sharkskin suits, a little something to scorch her throat. Drawn to the jukebox, she punches one letter, one number, and "This Bitter Earth" punches her back, with its sad indigo spin. Dinah settles like storm over her shoulders. And she weeps when she hears what has happened to homemade guitars. How they've forgotten to need the Southern moon.

OTIS AND ANNIE, ANNIE AND OTIS

My parents, then

She's a gum-crackin', bowlegged, church-decent gal, raised up,
looks like, by a mama who prayed and aimed her toward right.
I feel a rumbling 'neath that skirt tho, some rhythm of city
she left Alabama with, a little bit of Chicago that chile
just couldn't keep outta her strut. Careful with this one, Otis,
cause that gold flashin' in her mouth ain't intended for God.
I'll dress like a real upright Christian for a few days, let her see
me sharp and crease up and smellin' sweet. I'll say *Annie*
like it's the first word I learned and the last one I'm gon' say.
But I won't be crossing the line, having that woman think
I'm the marryin' kind. She start dreamin' on a white dress
and babies wearin' my face. Lawd, that ain't what I want.

> Is there a life outside of Jesus? Then that's what I want,
> at least for a few days. Nights. I wanna put my hair up,
> pour myself into something shiny, open my mouth and say
> what I feel like sayin', for a change. Gon' buy me a gold dress
> with pearl buttons, a split up both sides. Cause I ain't a child
> no more, hanging onto Mama Ethel's hand. Next time you see
> me, you won't know who you're staring at, no way you look right
> past me. I'm an up-North woman now. It's about time Annie
> Pearl growed up, found work that ain't in dirt, learned some city
> words. Don't want nobody calling me *country*, folks thinkin'
> Alabama can't be shook off and thrown out. So I pray to God
> every night for that dress money. And maybe that man. He named Otis.

So I iron my good shirt, clean up, say "My name's Otis,"
and she smile behind her hand like she don't already know. I want
to just rush thangs and feel all my body pressed on her, but God

still a somebody in my head, and Annie Pearl still be His child.
So she's saying things I should be hearing, but all I can see
is stuff I'm not lookin' at—that rumble in her clothes, moon up
'gainst her skin, all that down-South brown looking just right
up here on the West Side. I know she a little scared of the city,
she dressed up like a big girl, putting on airs to make me think
she more woman than she is. But she woman enough. I say,
"You know, you look real pretty in that dress . . . ," though the dress
is plain, gray, and sewed flat. Then I add her name, ". . . Annie."

       I go a little crazy at the way he say my name. He say, "Annie"
       like it's the first word he learned. So I feel his name, Otis,
       in my mouth before it come out. Then I pull it out slow, and I see
       his eyes get real wide like he about to outright praise his God
       because of what I said and how I said it. Ain't gon lie, chile,
       that felt good. But I ain't foolin' myself—he ain't everything I want.
       Like me, he lookin' for some kinda job, living in his one room, and I think
       I might not be the only woman he talkin' to. But he'll do me right,
       and I sho need some kinda strong man stand beside me in this city,
       while I find me a church and someplace better to live, a real address
       where folks from down home can find me when they take the bus up.
       So I say, "I been watching you a long time." That's what I say.

So I'm trying not to look at what I'm not looking at, and she say,
all bold, "I been watching you a long time," and I say "Annie,
you sumthin' else, you know?" but what I'm thinkin' is, *God,
we stuck in this little talk.* "You know, Miss Annie Pearl, I think
we need to go someplace, have us some food, maybe up
there on Madison, someplace close like that chicken joint right
down the street from the tavern?" She smile and I swear I see
something I hope I see again, what I think I see is some child
in her, all worked up 'bout going someplace new in the city,
even a hole-in-the-wall with burnt wings most folks don't want.
She say, stiff like white folks, "I-really-would-like-that-Otis,"
but I see her frowning a little when she look down at her dress.

I woulda felt real slick walking into that chicken place in a dress
with pearl buttons and splits on both sides, but Otis grin and say
I look good in the dress I was in. That the first time I thank God
for him, even before I took him in my bed, tasted his mouth, I think
it was knowing he care 'bout me enough to lie, say I'm a pretty chile
when I'm not. I feed him with my fingers, let him eat fried bread right
off my plate while folks who know him whispering. I let them see
who he was gon' be with, the woman he was gon' be pressed up
'gainst from now on. Wanted to yell at them women "I'm the one he want!
Tell everybody you know, here and in Alabama too. My name is Annie,
and starting right now I want you to know that this is my man Otis."
Don't know what made me think crazy like that. Sounding like the city.

Done heard it before, and now I'm 'bout to believe that the big city
ain't no place for a woman and man. Every day, that woman got to dress
my wounds, hear about the ways I done got beat down, she get to see
my head bowed all the damned time. I really try not to show my Annie
how small I feel on the factory line, try not to let on how much I want
just for me, before I even *think* of me and her. Like a fool, she lift me up.
I'm steady riding her shoulders, promising the world. It ain't right,
that I can't give her what she's dreamin' on. I know she startin' to think
maybe I'm not the man who deserves her gold. I'm just a plain Otis—
damn if that ain't a country name—and at night I hear her ask God
for something more. I play cards, sip my JB, run out of things to say
to her. Cause she thinks a baby will save us. Lord, she wants a child.

I know, a woman got to be a natural fool to want to bring a child
into this mess of broke glass and nailed-up doors, this goddamn city.
That's right, country girl lose Jesus now and then, you heard me say
it, goddamn, sometime I close my eyes and can't feel my God.
I sit up at night, staring at them dirty city stars and waiting for Otis
to knock on my door. I don't have to wait long, never do, cause I think
that wherever he is he can feel me wanting. I hear him coming up
my stairs, seems like slower each time, and when I open the door I see
what I'm afraid I'll see, that maybe he got no idea at all what I really want.

Maybe I done gave up on them pretty pearl buttons, that shiny dress.
I don't touch him. He put his rough hands soft on my face, says "Annie,
you want all of me, think I'm a marryin' man? Then let's make it right."

I can't look in her eye, seeing all that lonely, and think I got a right
to keep being me instead of doin' right by the bowlegged 'bama chile
I talked into loving me. My heart 'bout blows up when she say "Otis,
you mean it? You mean it?" And I hear myself say yes. I pick her up
and press her whole body to me and just for that second the city
disappears, Chicago and all its lies are gone, and I say "Annie,
you need to be my wife," and I know I'm sayin' it just so I won't see
that longing in her no more. I can't believe I was fool enough to think
I could have my drink and my fast city women, then come home, say
"Baby, it's hard out there," and she would hold me, wearing that dress
that's plain, gray, and sewed flat, and that all she'd ever want
was just that—a cheater in her arms, steady making his promises to God.

I don't know how I'm gon' handle this thick in my body, God,
without Otis knowing it. He's gon' be a father, and he sho' got a right
to know that, to know that our lives gon' be changed way before we say
them vows, he got a right to know how many ways this big ol' city
gon' get harder for us, the three of us. When he come home, say "Annie,
it's gon' be all right," he talking just 'bout just me and him—he adding up
our money every week, trying to cut down on the times he see
his other women, coming home for dinner most every night. Otis
is probably somebody's daddy already, somewhere, so why I think
this gon' hit him so hard? Maybe it's because I think this child
is gon' be everything we have—I'll feed it, rock it to sleep, dress
it in pink or blue and pretend that it's all we ever gon' want.

So it look like Annie Pearl 'bout to get just what she want.
I done seen pregnant women before, how they walk, cry how God
suddenly got a place in everything they say. I sit her down, say "Annie,
I ain't no boy. And I ain't no fool either. I know you carryin' a chile,
and I know that chile is mine. Folks have babies all the time in the city,

just like they did down South. Sure as my given name is Otis,
I'm gon' be here with you, do you right, and I'm gon' have a say
in how this child grows." I know she scared. I know she think
I might be the wrong man, that I can't hold still, and she right
'bout that, but a chile can make a man change. We gon' fix up
our lives, make a place for this baby. I'm gon' get her that gold dress
'fore she get big, before her belly out there for everybody to see.

Otis could be the wrong man. So many folks saying I need to see
that. So I pray on it. Most times, he's just a little of everything I want.
When he don't come home for two, three nights, I ask God
to change his ways, or at least keep him alive. When this hungry city
open its mouth and he walk in again, I got no idea what words to say
to get him home. When I hear 'bout them other women, how they dress
tight, wear red lips and laugh with their mouths wide open, how Otis
spend money on that laughing, how he rock me soft, saying "Annie,
baby, it's hard out there," while I get bigger and bigger with this chile,
I just cry. And then I scream. Cause there's this pain like a knife slice right
where my baby supposed to be. Whether that man here or not, I think
this 'bout to happen. Chile moving fast, not giving me time to catch up.

Whenever I think about Otis and Annie, two stars orbiting the city,
there's no way I can say how they found each other. But I can see
how the child who became Patricia Ann is equal parts of both of them.
Otis and Annie, maybe with the help of some fool's God, etched a road right
up Chicago's middle and placed a confounded child there. And that gold dress
that Otis, my daddy, promised his Alabama girl? It never stopped being a want.

JUNE 25, 1955

in the hospital

It is a backbreaker delivery, with no knife *cut the pain of*
slipped beneath the bed to cut the pain. *pregnancy*
In a deep-bleached cavern of beeping
machines and sterilized silver, she can't
get loose. Her legs are strapped flat,
and men are holding down her hands.
She wails. Not from hurt, but from knowing. *what does*
There will be no running from this. *she know?*
This child is a chaos she must name.

childbirth?

14

SHOULDA BEEN JIMI SAVANNAH

My mother scraped the name Patricia Ann from the ruins
of her discarded Delta, thinking it would offer me shield
and shelter, that leering men would skulk away at the slap
of it. Her hands on the hips of Alabama, she went for flat
and functional, then siphoned each syllable of drama,
repeatedly crushing it with her broad, practical tongue
until it sounded like an instruction to God, not a name.
She wanted a child of pressed head and knocking knees,
a trip-up in the doubledutch swing, a starched pinafore
and peppermint in the sour pickle kinda child, stiff-laced
and unshakably fixed on salvation. *Her* Patricia Ann
would never idly throat the Lord's name or wear one
of those thin, sparkled skirts that flirted with her knees.
She'd be a nurse or a third-grade teacher or a postal drone,
jobs requiring alarm-clock discipline and sensible shoes.
My four downbeats were music enough for a vapid life
of butcher-shop sawdust and fatback as cuisine, for Raid
spritzed into the writhing pockets of a Murphy bed.
No crinkled consonants or muted hiss would summon me.

My daddy detested borders. One look at my mother's
watery belly, and he insisted, as much as he could insist
with her, on the name Jimi Savannah, seeking to bless me
with the blues-bathed moniker of a ball breaker, the name
of a grown gal in a snug red sheath and unlaced All-Stars.
He wanted to shoot muscle through whatever I was called,
arm each syllable with tiny weaponry so no one would
mistake me for anything other than a tricky whisperer
with a switchblade in my shoe. I was bound to be all legs,
a bladed debutante hooked on Lucky Strikes and sugar.
When I sent up prayers, God's boy would giggle and consider.

Daddy didn't want me to be anybody's surefire factory,
nobody's callback or seized rhythm, so he conjured
a name so odd and hot even a boy could claim it. And yes,
he was prepared for the look my mother gave him when
he first mouthed his choice, the look that said, *That's it,
you done lost your goddamned mind.* She did that thing
she does where she grows two full inches with righteous,
and he decided to just whisper *Love you, Jimi Savannah*
whenever we were alone, re- and rechristening me the seed
of Otis, conjuring his own religion and naming it me.

CHICAGO

After Carl Sandburg

SOUL   Butcher for the Country,
         Heartbreaker, Stacker of the Deck,
         Player with Northbound Trains, the Nation's Black Beacon;
         Frigid, windy, sprawling,
         City of Cold Shoulders.

They tell me you have lied and I believe them,
for I have seen your Mississippi women stumbling
Madison Street searching for their painted city legs.

And they tell me you are evil and I answer: Yes, I know.
I have seen babies cooking their hair, fingering blades,
changing their names to symptoms of jazz.

And they speak of souls you swallow, and my reply is:
On the shadowed faces of men in the factory lines
I have witnessed the beginnings of the furthest falling.

And having answered so I turn to the people who spit at my city,
and I spit back at them before I say:

Come and show me another city with head thrown back wailing
    bladed blue, field hollers, so astounded to be breathing and bleeding.
Spewing electric hymns rhythmed against the staccato pound of
    fiery steel presses, here is a defiant ass whupper
    shaking its massive fists at sweating southern "towns";

Feral as a junkyard mutt, taut, muscled against his enemy, shrewd
    as an explorer pitted against an untried land,

Wily as a Louisiana boy faced with days of concrete,
     Wiry-headed,
     Digging,
     Destroying,
     Deciding,
     Swallowing, expelling, swallowing,

Under the rubble, thrusting forth, laughing with
    perfect teeth,
Shedding the terrible burden of skin, laughing as a white
    man laughs,
Laughing even as a soldier laughs, addicted to the need of his next battle,
Laughing and bragging that under that skin is the cage of his ribs
And under his ribs beats a whole unleashed heart.
             Laughing!
Laughing the frigid, windy, sprawling laughter of
    a Southern man, folded against the cold, sparkling, sweating,
    proud to be
SOUL   Butcher for the Country,
       Heartbreaker, Stacker of the Deck,
       Receiver of Northbound Trains and the Nation's Black Beacon.

TEПZOПE

Chicago to Patricia Ann

Can I help it that my maw is shaped
exactly like your body, that my fists
ache for the shake of you? Now you've been scraped
from Alabama womb, I can't resist
your dumb unfurling. You beg me to be
your father, or your mother sporting breasts
of dime-store glass. My trusting refugee,
I really have to say, I'm unimpressed
by you. I idly sniff the sugared fat
around your heart, decide that I'll combat

what's soft—your pulsing light, that wretched tune
that's building in your chest. Hey, take a look
around. This ain't no lush, no warm cocoon,
no mama's coo. You and your kind mistook
my glitter for consent, my unsnapped trap
for open arms. I'm only jukebox skin
and towered brick, a shifting god who'll slap
you back to birth, girl, don't you think this grin
means anything but glee. I own you now—
that Northern star's no beacon anyhow.

So don't you worry, child, I'll raise you right.
I'll skin your knees, I'll soil your pirouette,
and whet your nasty little appetite
for light in alleyways. I'll make you sweat
it out, that fever that so glorified
your coming here. Your parents' naked dream,

19

that laughable and misdirected pride,
that harboring of points they can't redeem,
that cramming all their faith in the debut
of something damned and weak. They named it you.

Patricia Ann to Chicago

Can I help the fact that I escaped,
exactly as they'd hoped, and that I missed
what Delta held for me? I saw you, draped
in textures I didn't think could coexist—
steel and heat and blended silks. The key
to loving you is knowing that you've dressed
in lies to tempt the travelers. *Oh, SweetPea,*
mama says, *child, know that you been blessed.*
She sends me stumbling out into the flat
light of your clutching moon, my habitat

assured—the dingy parks, the alleys strewn
with glittered garbage, every cozy nook
shaped like astonished little girl. And soon,
aloud, you say my name—the shiny hook
of Northwashed noun, the awkward sound a gap
in air. Declaring us a fractured kin,
you vow me yours. Our heartbeats overlap
as you instill your loving discipline.
I learn to breathe the blue that you allow,
to readjust my history somehow.

My clanging harbor, almost overnight
you've wooed me with the terrifying threat
of bustling where I'm not. I crave your bite,
the way your every touch tends to reset

my temperature, that strut you strut beside
me, arcing, shielding, sewing shut that seam
where light leaks in. I'm one child, magnified,
so many of us, thousands, suddenly seem
so snug within your arms. I weep on cue.
I finally found religion, named it you.

3315 W. WASHINGTON, 3A

This is heartbeat now—shadowbox, dinette
purchased with slow nickels, skittering mice
wedged beneath the stove, warbling their regret
like balladeers. This patchwork paradise

smells vaguely of impending sacrifice
and admissions of defeat. Better yet,
it stinks of chance, the brash tossing of dice.
This is heartbeat now—shadowbox, dinette,

paid for on time, such fashionable debt
for thin and collapsible merchandise
that's prayed for, then thrown out. A safety net
purchased with slow nickels. Skittering mice

know no one will heed their feverish advice
even as they croon in doomed, blue quartet.
Their soundtrack of the slum, fractured, concise,
intent beneath the stove, is warbled regret.

Again, Chicago's perfect silhouette
reshapes the room, pretties up to entice
the migrants, who sing city alphabet
like balladeers. That patchwork paradise

has vowed to save them—a jumble of vice
and lies, northward promise, remembered sweat
and sometimes dead mice might have to suffice
before the revelation of sunset.
This is heartbeat now.

ALLIANCE

All I wanted that year was one of those tall blonde
dolls, always pale-named Susie something, a doll
that bolted forward *("She's magic! She walks! She
looks just like you!")* when you squeezed her hand
just so, one of those dolls with flat nightmare hair
the color of exploded corn and a dress that glowed
and crinkled and sparked. I wanted a perfect friend
to stumble ahead with, an unyielding plastic to wrestle
and wake against, all I wanted was blue flutter-lashed
eyes flapping little voodoo, I wanted to fall in love
with and be horrified by her, to search her mouth
for a full tongue, to grow to resent her, to grant her
mysticism and fury, to lock her up in my closet and
watch the doorknob all damn night, waiting for that
slow *Twilight Zone* twist. All I talked was Susie this,
Susie that, scrawling her in tortured block-lettered
pleadings with Santa, taking my father by the hand
and leading him past rows and rows of her shelved
at Kresge's. I said I'd never ever ask for anything
else again ever, not knowing that Barbie, just one
aisle over, was sharpening her fashionable talons,
sniffing the air for fresh breasts and menstrual blood.
I wanted, wanted and prayed for something hard
and possible. My fresh mute walking baby woman.

But on Christmas Eve, when I snuck a peek through
my wishing window into the starry, slanted snow
and saw Daddy pull a want-shaped box from the trunk
of his Buick, it didn't stun my belief in the annual
gospel of a porky, apple-cheeked Santa. You know,

I wasn't stupid—at eight, I'd already signed on for
the miraculous black art of white men. They danced
in my cereal, sold detergent to my mother, this one
shimmied down tenement chimneys. I knew Santa
was still coming, tugged by huffing reindeer, fooled
again by my wide-eyed vow that I'd been an angel.
This gift came from another place, for another reason.

I folded my little body into the dark, kept watching.
When I glimpsed pink knees and a sunshiny coif
through the box's cellophane front, I thought it was
only right that my father loved hard enough to introduce
Susie to the dim, resigned sigh of his daughter. All that
frosted night, they must have huddled, plastic against
pulse, discussing my sad soft, the out-loud mistakes
in my walking. Actually, only my father spoke. Susie
simply nodded, her stout legs thrumming, a warm
purpose trembling behind her slammed-shut tempera smile.

2

WE SHINED LIKE THE NEW THINGS WE WERE

A COLORED GIRL WILL SLICE YOU
IF YOU TALK WRONG ABOUT MOTOWN

The men and women who coupled, causing us, first
arrived confounded. Surrounded by teetering towers
of *no, not now,* and *you shoulda known better,* they
cowered and built little boxes of Northern home,
crammed themselves inside, feasted on the familiar
of fat skin and the unskimmed, made gods of doors.
When we came—the same insistent bloody and question
we would have been down South—they clutched us,
plumped us on government cereal drenched in Carnation,
slathered our hair, faces, our fat wiggling arms and legs
with Vaseline. We shined like the new things we were.
The city squared its teeth, smiled oil, smelled the sour
each hour left at the corner of our mouths. Our parents
threw darts at the day. They romanced shut factories,
waged hot battle with skittering roaches and vermin,
lumbered after hunches. Their newborn children grew
like streetlights. We grew like insurance payments.
We grew like resentment. And since no tall sweet gum
thrived to offer its shouldered shade, no front porch
lesson spun wide to craft our wrong or righteous,

our parents loosed us into the crumble, into the glass,
into the hips of a new city. They trusted exploded
summer hydrants, scarlet licorice whips, and crumbling
rocks of government cheese to conjure a sort of joy,
trusted joy to school us in the woeful limits of jukeboxes
and moonwash. Freshly dunked in church water, slapped
away from double negatives and country ways, we were

orphans of the North Star, dutifully sacrificed, our young
bodies arranged on sharp slabs of boulevard. We learned
what we needed, not from our parents and their rumored
South, but from the gospel seeping through the sad gap
in Mary Wells's grin. Smokey slow-sketched pictures
of our husbands, their future skins flooded with white light,
their voices all remorse and atmospheric coo. Little Stevie
squeezed his eyes shut on the soul notes, replacing his
dark with ours. Diana was the bone our mamas coveted,
the flow of slip silver they knew was buried deep beneath
their rollicking heft. Every lyric, growled or sweet from
perfect brown throats, was instruction: *Sit pert, pout, and
seamed silk. Then watch him beg.* Every spun line was
consolation: *You're such a good girl. If he has not arrived,
he will.* Every wall of horn, every slick choreographed
swivel, threaded us with the rhythm of the mildly wild.
We slept with transistor radios, worked the two silver knobs,
one tiny earbud blocking out the roar of our parents' tardy
attempts to retrieve us. Instead, we snuggled with the Temps,
lined up five pretty men across. And damned if they didn't
begin every one of their songs with the same word: *Girl*.

ANNIE PEARL'S ARETHABOPS

She wakes up to the radiating of his curved body
snapped to hers. Not wanting his eyes to open yet,
she resists the urge to shift too suddenly toward
the smudged window, its unwelcoming sun. Instead
she links to the clock of his breathing, sniffs its sour
relentless cream. Again, she'd dreamed of slapping him.

One morning that chain is gonna break.
'Til then, I'm gonna take all I can take.

How could he have saved her so deftly, charging
up on a stallion the color of West Side slush, lifting
her off her feet, vowing screwtop wine and reversals?
Eventually Chicago would demand to be romanced,
switching her formidable hip to a raucous duet
of marked cards and mistaken clocks. Now, when
he locks onto her eyes and mentions love, he sputters
hollows. The O of his practiced mouth, still perfect.

One morning that chain is gonna break.
'Til then, I'm gonna take all I can take.

She finds the suitcase in the hall closet; still clinging
to their first unfolding. It stinks of Alabama. While
he sleeps, snorting in fractures, she tosses in wingtips,
unmatched cufflinks, a Luckys pack, a pewter
sharkskin suit, his ashed cantata hands, those lips.
Aloud, she says *I love you.* Then forgets why.

One morning that chain is gonna break.
'Til then, I'm gonna take all I can take.

2.

Get out! Her hair conks rivers, her eyes bulge.
It doesn't help that he is smiling sad crooked sugar,
doesn't help that he watches her raving from
beneath hooded lids, mumbling *Girl, c'mon now*
like she is just a hardheaded cur straining the leash.
He says no way he's leaving. She bares her teeth.

No-good heartbreaker; you're a liar, you're a cheat—
I don't know why. I let you do these things to me . . .

She thinks of his burnt-orange women, puff-lipped,
deep-spritzed beehives, wiggled seams snaking down
the backs of their legs, sadiddy asses dripping off
the edges of barstools while he spoon-feeds them spirits
and meat. She thinks of mouths thrown open, red octave
cackles riding a surface of glass. And his hands on them,
unthreading her language. Their hurried names, written
in whiskey, had sweated out the lining of his pocket.

No-good heartbreaker; you're a liar, you're a cheat—
I don't know why. I let you do these things to me . . .

I ain't going nowhere woman, and she sways,
considers regretting, as he turns his wall of a back
to the unsettled weather of her. Instead, she folds,
grows small, hard, a brusque knot of what she was.
She flashes her bricked torso, and he skips a beat
in his breath. She could carry his ass out, and would.

No-good heartbreaker; you're a liar, you're a cheat—
I don't know why. I let you do these things to me . . .

3.

Back when Alabama was a quick hot glance over
her shoulder, when Arkansas numbed his calling
tongue, they emerged, stumbling, from the exhaust
of northbound buses and coupled on the warped
hardwood of that first home. There was only the one
and the one. Always the denying there would be others.

My soul was in the lost and found.
You came along to claim it.

Imagine a savior not being forever. She had stitched
her whole self to his forward, forward, his angled
shoulders. Her tenement body craved his cures,
the gospel of his denying nouns. And he said *woman*
then, and he meant her, the way she was, thick
and Southern. Remembering, she engines beneath him
a final time, grieving, annoyed by his familiar burn.
Aloud, he says *Thank you, baby.* Silent, she says good-bye.

My soul was in the lost and found.
You came along to claim it.

Bellowed rebuttals, his shirt still off, chest scarred by
the screeched road of a bitten, unpolished fingernail, one
fevered *You crazy, bitch?* unanswered in the air, suddenly
it's all grind and blue juke, another English he has learned.
He bangs and shivers the thin doorframe on the way out,
stunning the stubborn beat of the thing he had rescued.

My soul was in the lost and found.
You came along to claim it.

TRUE THAT

In my neighborhood
I got jumped
because my daddy lived at home.
Then,
when he didn't live at home anymore,
I got jumped
because he had the nerve
to visit.

SHEDDING

She screamed when she saw the clumps of hair
in my hand, the slowly uncrumpling wads stuffing
the sink drain, the nappy tufts clinging to the slick
white walls of the tub. In disbelief, she dragged
her claw across my scalp, then stared at the thick
tendrils that easily came away with her hand.
"Girl, what did you *do?*" she demanded, deciding
that the loss of my hair was punishment for some
closeted purple sin, so then began the questions:
*Did you let anybody touch you? You been going
to school every day? Have you been stopping off
at that place where they sell candy? Girl, you been
stealing stuff from Woolworth's, slipping money
outta my purse? Did you say something wrong
to God? You call God out His name? You been
cursing?* I was eight. Nothing purple could find
thread in me. All I knew was that the week before,
my mother had stated, casually, while she chopped
onions or tuned in to *Petticoat Junction* or shaved
a corn on her toe with a razor, "Oh, your daddy
ain't gonna be living here no more," and my halo
shredded and my whole slice of sky started to hurt.

LAUGH YOUR TROUBLES AWAY!

Motto, Riverview Park, 1904–1967, Chicago

I.

Every city had one, a palace with a fried tint to its air,
a hurting-hued screech of no underneath, everything
plummeting or ascending, a monument to hazy flailing
and sudden fun vomit. Swing the Riviera onto Belmont,
and you see the Pair-O-Chutes rising to heaven on dual
strings, headed for the pinpoint and release, then the sick
whip and fall, the little public murder, a blaring grace
so storybook gorgeous, suddenly flood in the throat.

Revelers board creaking Fireball cars and slice the August,
mistaking acid bubbling in their bellies for symptoms
of glee, then stop to stuff quavering guts with plastic
and syrup. Their quick sustenance has wafted all day
all day on a river of grease. They hunger for white cakes
curled stiff with sugar, sausages that pop huge heat,
pink candy of cotton chomping rot down their throats.
The jagged stains of compromised fruit circle screaming
mouths and paint shadow across the teeth, making them
horrible. Bulbs flash. Wet Polaroids are lifted and waved
like church fans to etch and clarify in the summer steam.

The aged horses are dizzied, diseased. Chained to a tilting
stake, they blur through the drag, deferring to their brutal,
squirming burdens. Potbellied flies, nasty to the point
of charm, nibble passages toward the horses' blue hearts.
Above it all, the freak show M.C.—his shout an odd mixture

34

of pity and sex—dares us to witness sweaty sloth, tiny floating
corpses, so much skin unlike ours, more legs than allowed,
and a Negro who can separate himself from his eyes.

While on the midway, your father will never win the thinly
stuffed neon grinners—the bears, dolphins, curlique serpents,
Kewpie dolls, and counterfeit Mickey Mice that leer from shelves.
He hurls balls at weighted milk cans, blasts at a measured parade
of bobbing ducks, guns water into a pinpoint, guesses a woman's
weight. Finally, he just buys something soft and ugly, a token
you will clutch and sing to until, too blackly loved, it melts.

At dusk, he steers you away from the midway's squalling edge,
where everything seems to be happening, where the hooting
and laughter have a raw, unmeasured throat. You pout, he pulls,
and, not for the first time, you wonder what he hides.

2.

I am their pickaninny, dressed in a repeating river.
All of me is droop and sustain.
My drenched dungarees are gravity on me.
I have learned to smile at the several versions
of my name, my face is complete in its teeth.
and studied dumb ogle. *Oh, woe is me* I say
while the white boys wind up, and damn if they
don't always smack that huge disc, dead center.
I rise laughing from my clockwork baptisms,
the canned river funked with my own spit and piss,
just to see another man clutching the red ball,
his eyes harder than the first of these. Sometimes
an awed Negro dots the crowd, his numbed smile

a link chained to mine. I spot one using his body
to block his little girl's view of me, so I make
my voice louder: I *oh sweet jesus kind suh no,*
I *lawd ham mercy suh* I *I believes I might drown*
I *please let me dry off in this sun a little* I *mercy*
me you sho does look strong suh until she twists
hard away from her daddy and full unto me.
I have just enough time for her to sound it out:
D-D-D-unk-unk Dunk a N-N-N-ig-ig-Nig-ger
and then I salute, and hold her father's eyes as I fall.

THE BOSS OF ME

In fifth grade I
was driven wild by you,
my teacher   Copper pixie
with light shining from beneath
it   Eyes giggling azure through
crinkled squint   I
let you rub my hair   I
let you probe the kinks   I
clutched you, buried my nose
in the sting starch of your white
blouses I asked you if you thought
I was smart did you know
how much I wanted to come
home with you to roll and cry on
what had to be a bone-colored
carpet I found out where
you lived I dressed in the morning
with you in mind I spelled huge
words for you I opened the dictionary
and started with *A* I wanted to
impress the want out of you
I didn't mind my skin because you
didn't mind my skin I opened big books
and read to you and watched TV news
and learned war and weather for you
I
needed you in me enough to take
home enough to make me stop rocking
my own bed at night enough
to ignore my daddy banging on the front door

and my mama not letting him in I
prayed first to God and then to you
first to God and then to you
then to you and next to God then
just to you
Mrs. Carol
Baranowski do you even remember
the crack of surrender under your hand?
Do you remember my ankle socks
kissed with orange roses, socks turned perfectly
down and the click of the taps in my black
shiny shoes that were always pointed toward
you always walking your way always
dancing for a word from you? I looked
and looked for current that second
of flow between us but our oceans
were different   yours was wide and blue
and mine
was

3

LEARNING TO SUBTRACT

OOO, BABY, BABY

A Smokey limerick on the long-play

There once was a song that took hold
of a child, cause the tale that it told
made her feel flushed and held
until she was compelled
to play it again, to behold
the craving encased in each note
that slipped from the singer's sleek throat—
cause the beg that he sighed
made her ache from inside.
She was moved by his words to devote
her tomorrows to all that he said.
She was told she was out of her head.
But his tenor dug deep,
interrupting her sleep,
so she did some wild dreaming. Instead
of singing it dizzy, she would
pretend that he loved her, or could.
In her mirror, she braced
for his kiss, and the taste
of his mouth. Every day, there she stood
in a room by herself, all alone
with a body no longer her own.
All her soul was engrossed
in no more than a ghost,
every moment a new stepping stone
toward an empty she didn't dare to name,
knowing Smokey was never to blame
though she whispered, *No fair*

as she slow-danced with air,
her hip-heavy waltzing a shame.
But if the song made her prefer
the conjure, the hot him and her,
she would live in her head,
stunned in love, newly wed,
the real just a feverish blur.
So she drowned in the silk of his voice
just because there was never a choice.
She was helplessly shook
by his *ooh la la* hook,
not a thing left to do but rejoice
in a romance that really was none
and a two that was really just one.
She was fatally awed
by a falsetto god—
his wooing had left her undone.
There once was a song that took hold
of a child, cause the story it told
made her feel flushed and held
until she was compelled
to give in to the lies that it sold.

FIRST FRICTION

I was twelve, too young to be left alone mornings
after Mama packed her paper hat and sugar-dusted
shoes to push gumballs down the assembly line.
So I was unceremoniously dumped at the door
of old Mrs. Gore's mouse-addled basement hovel,
where the matron of snapping gum and gray grin
ushered me in and plopped me down in a chair
that stank of a dog they didn't own. Seeing how I was
bleary and unslept, Mrs. Gore would open the door
to the bedroom where her twin girls, Kathy and Karen,
still dreamed on the edge of alarm. Peppery, flailing,
their waking bodies unwound to carve me room.
I don't know how it started, how, wordlessly, Karen
and I tussled skin, adjusted knee and cunt, naturally
knew the repeating mouth and its looping stanza.
She smelled like what I couldn't stop swallowing.
Content to thrive on a flickering cinema of ourselves,
our eyes fluttered, never fully opened. We pretended
a blazing slumber, hushing the grind, the soft rustle
of sparse sweating pubic, even after her unsuspecting
sister stretched and tumbled out to begin her day.
Strange she didn't suspect our engine. For as long
as we could, Karen and I stayed prone in exquisite,
pressurized tangle beneath the knotty orange chenille.
We kept up the being blind, crashing into dampening
borders, until her fat mother shuffled in to rouse us,
throwing shades open to the damnable day, introducing
the stupid, useless notion of language again. By then,
there was a drum buried in our bellies. We stank like
men, all up under that sweet funk first sin leaves behind.

SPECULATION

Thirty years after Richard Speck murdered eight nurses on the South Side of Chicago, videotapes surfaced showing the convicted killer in prison parading in silk panties and sporting breasts reportedly grown with smuggled hormone treatments. After talking about the rampant sex he enjoyed, he said, "If they only knew how much fun I was having, they'd turn me loose."

I.

Of course, you're everybody's bitch now,
your face aunt-soft, but still pummeled
and pitted, still that drooped dammit
of marbled landscape. Of course you are
slouch and winking sloe-eyed beneath
a Dutch-boy bowl of hair, pert pouted
areolas lazed on a pimpled gut, this is
what happens when eight women insist
on a winter rhythm inside you, they bless
you with feminine clock, sly locomotion,
with the hips they were just beginning.
With fabled cock crumpled backways
in panties of silk dark as a blue note,
you rise to walk, focused, overclicking
your sway like a practiced hag on the stroll
while, nodding gravely behind aviator
shades, your Negro lover wryly considers
the sashaying, ill-constructed hot mass
murderer mess of you. He is overseer,
brusque pimp. You are his gilded tunnel.
Between demanded fevers, you amuse him.

How'd it feel when you killed them ladies?
he monotones, in reluctant acknowledgment
of your stardom, your skewed rep, never
lifting his eyes to the camera, and of course
you had to say that you didn't feel anything—
It's just wasn't their night—nothing at all
when the fatty spit in your face and said
she'd remember everything about the way
you looked, nothing as the screeching parade
of cheekbone and thigh turned your quest
for pocket change into a giddy little fuck/slice,
nothing after finding out that the little Filipino
whore had rolled under the bed to memorize
your ruined skeletal grace, foolishly denying
herself the impossible Wednesday of you.

2.

I was nine when your pebbled hangdog filled
the face of the family Philco. No one prepared me.
I nibbled sardines and saltines and twisted
the torsos of dolls while staring at the lineup
of neat nurses you had romanced and ended,
pictures always in the same order, all your girls
sporting puffed bouffants and hard white collars
buttoned to a point above their throats, and I
studied their faces, a tomorrow all expectant and
persistent in them. They were my first dead girls.
I practiced their names over and again, loving
Matusek's white suburban splatter, the wide lyric
of *Merlita Garguilo*. In 1966, my parents, just
about a decade north, had clearly been deceived.

I was often alone with the perfect magic box,
Lucy and Vietnam one and the same, so no one
explained the frayed edges of narrative, grainy
shots of red-drenched beds, and you, you,
greasy pompadour, batter-skinned, droop-lipped
and lanky, my first killer within walking distance.
But before I knew what you wanted that night,
years before the televised daybreak of woman
in you, I was nine. You were always all over me.
I fell asleep under my Murphy bed, curled hard
against you, holding my own neck in my hands.

JUMPING DOUBLEDUTCH

Calves go chaos under pounding,
clothesline raises welt and bloodies
shin and ankle, hip and forearm
while we throw down nasty verses
and the boys step from the shadows.
In our stanzas, swerving beckons,
all our skin is steam and shining,
and we're women—not these babies
spouting bowlegs, stomping rhythm,
not these braids of quick unravel.
Hear our keyless, tangled trochees—
Butch and Sally in the alley.
Squeeze them titties like you mean it.
Bet you ain't gon' reach my panties!
Jump and whirl, we tempt our future
in a language born of beatdown,
verbs we urge from high-top sneakers.
Whipping hips and licking lips and
punishing the ground with craving,
got no notion what we're asking.
Mamas screeching from the windows,
Chile, you better stop that jumping,
showin' the neighborhood your business!
Bring your tail inside for dinner!
And the boys slide from the shadows.

MINUS ONE. MINUS ONE MORE.

Carol Burnett tugs an ear, waves toodly-doo to the camera eye.
It's ten o'clock, and a white mechanized man asked if I, a child,
know where my children are. No, but it's time for the news, time
for the insisting war, and the preposterous Philco—half monster
TV screen, half bulky, functional phonograph—blares jungle, its
flat glass face filled with streaked pans of crushed foliage, the whir
of blades, dust-dreary GIS heaving through quick-slamming throats.
Lurching toward the ledges of copters, they screech commands,
instructions, prayers, struggle to cram blooded lumps back into
their uniforms—*dead there, there, let's see, almost dead over there*—
a hand dangling by tendrils, a left eye imploded, black-and-white
red etches slow roadways into the back of a dimming hand. Beneath
the lack of hue, a white buzz, a lazy scroll of dates and numbers:
This is how many gone today, how many last week, last month,
this year. Big Daddy Cronkite's eyes glaze, consider closing, refocus.

Think of all the children plopped in front of this unscripted boom
to pass the time. Think of Tom turning Jerry's head into spectacular
dust, then this, our first official war smashing into the family room,
blurring into cinema, into lesson. It's how we learned to subtract.

AND NOW THE NEWS: TONIGHT THE SOLDIERS

dropped their guns to dance. The sight
of spinning starlit men, their arms
around such waiting waists, alarmed
those paid to blare the urgent words
of war. And how did these hard men
decide on just this time to twirl
in bloodied dust, and how do we
explain the skin to skin, their hips
aligned, dramatic dips—*was that*
a kiss? Some rumba, others throw
a soundtrack down—they pound deep drums,
they twang imagined strings, they blow
notes blasted blue through sandy winds,
they dream a stout piano's weight.
They spark the dance—the bop and twist,
the tango, yes, the trot, the stroll,
the slither-slow unmanly grind
within a brother's brazen arms.
The talking heads can't spit enough
as cameras catch the swirling men,
their thrown-back heads and bended backs,
the rhythm of their rite, the ways
they steam. The toothy anchors chant
the traitors' numbers, names, to shame
them into still. But still the music
blows, the soldiers pivot, swing,
unleash their languid limbs, caress.
They don't slow down to weep or stop
to grieve their new-gone guns. The public
bray begins, *the song of killers*

killing must resume! but then
the mirthful moon illuminates
the ball, our boys in dip and glide
and woo. We see the dancers' dangling
eyes and blaring open sores,
shattered shoulders, earlobes smashed,
the halves of heads, the limp, the drag
of not quite legs. The soldiers dropped
their guns, and snagged a nasty bass
to roughride home. You hear the stomp,
the weary wheeze and grunt, the ragged
nudge of notes on air? You see
the whirling soldiers spin, the love
they braved, and oh my god, that kiss?

HAVE SOUL AND DIE

For Mary Wells

Stiff wigs, in cool but impossible shades
of strawberry and sienna, all whipped
into silky flips her own flat naps could
never manage—the night hair different
from the day hair, the going out hair,
the staying-in hair, Friday's hair higher
and way redder than Monday's—all these
wigs, *100% syn-the-tic, thank you,* lined
up on snowy Styrofoam heads and paid
for with her own money, what could be
slicker than that? No lovesick player
flopped his wallet open for *those* crowns.

So she wasn't Diana. Who wanted to be
all skeleton and whisper, hips like oil?
Didn't need no hussies slinking in the
backdrop giving more throat, boosting
her rhythm. So what if her first album
cover drew her pimpled, bloat-cheeked,
Sunday hair skewed? She roared gospel
in those naked songs, took Berry's little
ballads and made men squirm on their
barstools. They spun her in the dark.

Wasn't she the alley grunt, the lyric played low?
Didn't people she never met run up to try
and own her tired shoulders, shouting *Mary!*
like they were calling on the mama of Jesus?

And everywhere she dared to step,
Detroit devilment bubbling beneath sequins
that can't help but pop under the pressure
black butts provide, every time she dropped
'round to paint the town brown, neon lights
slammed on, cameras clicked like air kisses,
and pretty soon somebody said *Girl you know*
you just gotta sing us something and even though
she didn't have to do a damned thing but be
black, have soul, and die, she'd puck those lips
just so, like she didn't know how damn electric
it all was, and every word landed torn and soft,
like a slap from somebody who loves you.

ΠEXT. ΠEXT.

he is the only white boy in lawndale
and who could blame him, searching
for a line of commerce that could save
his life? he starts hanging in the shadows
of our apartment building, pulling down
his pants and charging us a dime to look,
a quarter to touch. stubbed fingers, dingy,
pinkish, thumbing it. the slowly writhing
nub hooded and winking sly neon, *here,*
here, here, go on, touch it, go on be startled
by its whispered little rhumba, its soft
arrogance. the long line of wait, colored
and curious, snakes washington street
with giggles electric, our one stomach
throbbing with this stupid magic. white boy
shifts from Ked to Ked, corporate bigwig
under the overhang, and if not for his
clipped command—*Next. Next.*—we would
not even notice him attached to the thing.

three dimes sweaty in my fist. i'm two
unraveled braids, grape bubble gum smash,
newly baptized into the wrong world.
i do not know the name of my immediate
future, wouldn't recognize the hot snap
of the word *cock,* i don't have a clue
to that thing's unerring purpose. but ouch,
a vessel deep in me is already calling.
i move forward, impatient, my touch
outstretched for a stranger, blood money

straight from my hurt to his. still, i'm blue
with shame because i know I'm the only one:
he has to take my hand and guide it there.

4

MAD AT MY WHOLE DAMN FACE

AIN'T BUT ONE WAY HEAVEN MAKES SENSE

or, Annie Pearl Smith Explains the U.S. Space Program

First of all, y'all fools. See what's right in front of you,
then got folks telling you you ain't seeing what you
just saw, other folks saying you saw more than you did.
Heaven is where my Jesus live. Just one way to get there,
no great big shiny ship can rise up on that sacred. They think
they gon' look the Lord dead in his eye, asking questions
with nerve enough to wait for answers? No man gon' reach
down, just scoop up moon, even if Mr. Cronkite say he did.
Them white men way out in a desert somewhere, stumbling
round in them blowed-up suits with movie stuff back a' them,
laughing inside those glass heads. And colored folks *aahing*
and *oohing* like the number's in and they got money comin'.'
Chile, I sho' didn't raise you to be this much fool this fast.
People got to pray they way up. One small step ain't enough.

TAVERN. TAVERN. CHURCH. SHUTTERED TAVERN,

then Goldblatt's, with its finger-smeared display windows full
of stifled plaid pinafore and hard-tailored serge, each unattainable
thread cooing the delayed lusciousness of layaway, another church

then, of course, Jesus pitchin' a blustery bitch on every other block,
then the butcher shop with, hard to believe, the blanched, archaic head
of a hog propped upright to lure waffling patrons into the steamy

innards of yet another storefront, where they drag their feet through
sawdust and revel in the come-hither bouquet of blood, then a vacant
lot, then another vacant lot, right up against a shoe store specializing

in unyielding leather, All-Stars and glittered stacked heels designed
for the Christian woman daring the jukebox, then the what-not joint,
with vanilla-iced long johns, wax lips crammed with sugar water,

notebook paper, swollen sour pickles buoyant in a splintered barrel,
school supplies, Pixie sticks, licorice whips, and vaguely warped 45s
by Fontella Bass or Johnny Taylor, now oooh, what's that blue pepper

piercing the air with the nouns of backwood and cheap Delta cuts—
neck and gizzard, skin and claw—it's the chicken shack, wobbling
on a foundation of board, grease riding relentless on three of its walls,

the slick cuisine served up in virgin white cardboard boxes with Tabasco
nibbling the seams, scorched wings under soaked slices of Wonder,
blind perch fried limp, spiced like it's a mistake Mississippi don' made,

and speaking of, July moans around a perfect perfumed tangle of eight
Baptist gals on the corner of Kedzie and Warren, fanning themselves
with their own impending funerals, fluid-filled ankles like tree trunks

sprouting from narrow slingbacks, choking in Sears's best cinnamon-
tinged hose, their legs so unlike their arms and faces, on the other side
of the street is everything they are trying to be beyond, everything

they are trying to ignore, the grayed promise of government, twenty-five floors
of lying windows, of peeling grates called balconies, of yellow panties
and shredded diapers fluttering from open windows, of them nasty girls

with wide avenue hips stomping doubledutch in the concrete courtyard,
spewing their woman verses, too fueled and irreversible to be not
listened to and wiggled against, and the Madison Street bus revs its tired

engine, backs up a little for traction and drives smoothly into the sweaty
space between their legs, the only route out of the day we're riding through.

SANCTIFIED

Every night, my mother leaned over a chipped porcelain tub.
She dragged the crotch of the day's panties over a washboard.
The crotch of those panties was cleaned thin, shredded bright.
She poured heat onto the absence of stain, pressed, rattled
the room with scrubbing, squeezed without rinsing, draped
the stiff, defeated things over the shower rod. Naked and
bubbled from the waist down, she flipped on the faucet
at the sink, ran the hot water until every surface was slimy
with steam, splashed a capful of disinfectant—meant for soiled
floors and scarred walls—into a rubber bag, filled the bag
with scalding water. She sat on the toilet, spread her legs,
stared again at the strands of silver. She twisted a tube to
the bag, snaked the tube inside her body. The slowly spreading
burn said the day was ending in God's name. She threw back
her head and bellowed. On a hook, waiting, a white dress.

An All-Purpose Product

What surfaces can I use this product on?

ANSWER: Lysol may be used on hard, nonporous surfaces throughout your home. Lysol cleans, disinfects, and deodorizes regular and nonwax floors, nonwood cabinets, sinks, and garbage pails. For painted surfaces, it is recommended that the product first be tested in a small inconspicuous area.

Can Lysol be used in the kitchen?

ANSWER: Lysol may be used on countertops, refrigerators, nonwood cabinets, sinks, stovetops, and microwave ovens. For the bathroom, it may be used for tiles, tubs, sinks, and porcelain. And for all around the house, it may be used on floors, garbage cans, in the basement, and in the garage.

Can I use this inside my refrigerator?

ANSWER: Lysol may be used on the inside of a refrigerator. However, you must remove all food, and rinse well after using the product.

Can I use this to kill mold and mildew?

Yes. Lysol controls the growth of mold and mildew. It kills the mold, but removal of the stain associated with mold and mildew can sometimes be tough.

Can I use this to scrub the uncontrollable black from the surface of my daughter, to make her less Negro and somehow less embarrassing to me? She's like the hour after midnight, that chile is.

Why, yes. Begin with one Sears gray swirled dinette set chair, screeching across the hardwood on spindly steel legs. Place the offending child on the ruptured plastic of the seat. Demand that she bend her neck to grant you access to the damaged area. You know, of course, that black begins at the back of the neck. Grab a kitchen towel, a washcloth, or a sponge, and soak with undiluted Lysol concentrate.

Ignoring the howls of the impossibly Negro child, scrub vigorously until the offending black surrenders. There may be inflammation, a painful rebellion of skin, slight bleeding. This is simply the first step to righteousness. The child must be punished for her lack of silky tresses, her broad sinful nose, that dark Negroid blanket she wears. Layers of her must disappear.

PRECAUTIONARY STATEMENTS. DANGER: CORROSIVE TO EYES AND SKIN. HARMFUL IF SWALLOWED. Causes eye and skin damage. Do not get in eyes or on skin. Wear protective eyewear and rubber gloves when handling.

Woman, your mission is beyond this. You must clean the child, burn the Southern sun from her. If she squirms from the hurting, demand that she hold on to the sides of the chair. Soak towel or sponge with our patented holy water. Repeat application.

I have tried to understand PRECAUTIONARY STATEMENTS my mother DANGER: her hatred of this CORROSIVE TO EYES AND SKIN of the me that wears this HARMFUL IF SWALLOWED the monster she had CAUSES EYE AND SKIN DAMAGE the monster she wanted DO NOT GET IN EYES OR ON SKIN

Mama, can't you read it? You want me to read it to you? I can't help being my color! I am black, I am not dirty. I am black, I am not dirty, I am black, I am. Not. Dirty. What you have birthed upon me will not come off. My hair is black crinkled steel, too short to stay plaited. My ass is wide and will get wider. You can pinch my nose, but it will remain a landscape. You cannot reverse me. What is filthy to you will never be cleansed. There is only one thing you can

change

I am not dirty, I am black. I am not dirty, I am black, I am not black, I am dirty. I am dirty black, not black. I am black and dirty. Dirt is black. Black is dirty. You convinced me that I am what is wrong in this world. Scrub me right.

Bleed me lighter.

What is the difference between disinfection and sanitization? Why are there two different usage directions for each?

ANSWER: According to the Environmental Protection Agency, "disinfection" is killing more than 99.99% of germs on hard, nonporous surfaces in ten minutes, and may pertain to a number of different types of bacteria, viruses, and fungi. The EPA defines "sanitization" as killing 99.9% of bacteria in five minutes or less.

Lysol products achieve sanitization in 30 seconds.

29. 28. 27. 26. 25. 24. 23. 22. 21. 20. 19. 18. 17. 16. 15. 14. 13. 12. 11. 10. 9. 8. 7. 6. 5. 4. 3. 2. . . .

Done.

BABY OF THE MISTAKEN HUE

Baby of the mistaken hue, child of the wrong nose
with its measure unleashed, baby of the nappy knot,
I am your mother. Mad at your whole damned face,
I swear to the task of torching the regrettable Delta
from your disobeying braids. I pinch your breathing
shut to reteach the bone, smear guaranteed cream
on your pimpled forehead, chin, and cheeks. I am
the corrector. Soaking a kitchen towel with the blaze
of holy water, I consider just what you are naked,
recoil at the insistent patches of midnight blanketing
your skin and I scrub, scrub, push the hard heel
of my hand deep into the dark, coax cleansing
threads of blood to the stinging surface, nod gently
in the direction of your *Mama, don't!* I command
you to bend, to turn, to twist in the wobbly dinette
chair and reveal what hides from me, those places
on you that still insist on saying Negro out loud.
Remember how the nonbelievers screeched their
nonbelief at Jesus even as he laid his giving hands
upon them? One day you will comprehend the torch
I am. You will be burned smaller, lighter, ever closer
to the whiteness of my God, who loves you as you are.

BECAUSE

we sipped blood siphoned from grocery store grapes
Because matrons squinted at the dim crackling pages of hymnals
Because we obediently warbled exactly what we found there
Because spurting prompt hallelujahs was serious business
Because my mother's gilded tooth flashed when she begged
Because on Sundays we presented God with several options
Because Rev. Thomas's sick ankles were stiff and blue with fluid
Because his spat truths were mangled by bad tooth and spittle
Because he made seventy-two years move like some golden engine
Because Tony the choir director was, how you say it, a sissy
Because that old organ wailed like the B-side of a backslap
Because the pocked wooden floor left language on our knees
Because the rafters grew slimy with wailing, because, well,
because Judas, a pimp in blacklight, was smirking at Jesus again
Because somebody definitely acted up and conjured Mississippi
Because salt pork flailed in a skillet in the basement kitchen
Because Lawd knows we were all gon' be crazy hungry
Because the Holy Ghost was dawdling in the men's room
Because He had scanned the crowd and wasn't crazy about His odds
Because the grandbabies of freed slaves shimmied in their seats
Because every upright elder in the front row blathered with fever
Because crosses, unblessed with bodies, were everywhere
Because every one of those wooden T's bellowed something out loud
Because, just like last time, the fun-word-of-the-day was *sacrifice*
Because that sissy popped like a tear dripped on a red stovetop
Because he flowed our whole upturned voice from his fingers
Because worshippers with straightened hair wept slivers of Delta
Because we were a tangled mess of sanctified thighs and tongues
Because several instigators whispered *Just felt the Ghost come in*
Because Annie Pearl Smith's dazzled eyes got all-the-way wide

Because her numbed and hard-girdled waistline twisted in bliss
Because thick bodies hit the floor hard, squalling, convulsing,
Because prim ushers dug white-gloved fingers into her forearms
Because I had to gaze into the peppermint of my mother's wail
Because I questioned what soft, holy monster writhed inside her
Because I had once again been spared the slick sleight hand
of the devious divinity, because that twirling sissy and I
loved wrong and were loved wrong, because when Tony sniffed
haughty at the thrashing, collapsing congregation and whipped the choir
in the direction of flame, I felt the organ's bright asking drip like fuel
into the blood feeding my little hip. So I struck the match.

WHAT GARFIELD PARK KEPT SAYING

No one skated. Of course we couldn't.
We had very specific ideas about blades,
and our feet were never involved: My mother
absently sucked the loose gold that framed
her left front tooth while slicing into the thickness
of some pig for the necessity of supper. Daddy
carried a quick-flick razor in the side pocket
of pencil-legged pants, just waitin' for some
fool to get wide on whiskey, slyly palm the ace,
and get cut. In my room off of other rooms,
I danced slow around the edges of paper dolls,
scared to slip and slice recklessly into blonde flips
or perfect pink legs. The idea of chilly dance,
of a snowy felt skirt with flouncy curled hem,
of lacing up in stiff white leather and scissoring
gracefully on dirty ice past storefront preaching
and gin mills, of lifting up one leg and spinning
like a hot whisper and not even falling, the idea
was hurtful because one more time I had to reach
so far outside my own head to even think that way.

But from the layered gray greenness of the park,
a recorded monotone kicked in, 10 p.m. every night,
droning until dawn: *Danger. Do not go on the ice.*
Danger. Do not go on the ice. Oh, that's left over,
daddy said, from the days when young Jews twirled
gleefully into and out of the arms of one another,
passing time while their fathers coaxed thick music
from bulky phonographs and their mothers fiddled
with the perfection of place settings. At night, the ice,

suddenly more water than anything, impenetrable
beneath the moonwash, would lure them back.
The recording was a monotone lullaby meant to lull
them to sleep. Because sometimes a starlit skater
would crack the lying surface, flail beautifully,
scream into the pocket of dark, and drown.

——

During the day, I'd scurry past the line of swings
singing out their rust. Boys leaned toward my
running to whisper a symphony of the word *pussy*,
and frightened manless mothers arced like rooftops
over their ashy screeching children. I searched hard
for the lost rink, a golden gleam beneath the napped
weeds and slush. One time I thought I sensed a faint
outline, a soft bean-shaped impression, muted and
glamorous, but there was nothing to be resurrected,
no water to freeze and glisten and beckon. The metered
frost of the nightly warning rode uselessly on the air,
continuing to fracture the ghosted dreams of Negroes.

But deep in the thump of December, some of Garfield's
ice circles turned to mirrors. I was obsessed, standing
then stomping on them, pounding with my full weight,
jumping then smashing down, tempting the fate I'd
been warned about, one more place only beauty could reach.

TO KEEP FROM SAYING *DEAD*

For Gwendolyn Brooks

Winter, with its numbing gusts and giddy twists of ice,
is gone now. It's time for warmth again.
So where is Gwendolyn Brooks?
Its huge shoulders slumped, Chicago craves her hobble,
turns pissed and gray, undusts her name.

To know her,
you need to ride her city's wide watery hips,
you need to inhale an obscene sausage
smothered in gold slipping onions
while standing on a chaotic streetcross
where any jazz could be yours.
Walk the hurting fields of the West Side,
our slice of city burned to bones in '68:

Goldblatt's, the colored Bloomingdale's, gone.

Lerners, where we learned pinafore, gone.

No more havens for layaway, no more places
to plop down a dollar a week for P.F. Flyers
or wool jumpers with seams glued shut.
The meat market with its bloody sawdust, torched,
its Jewish proprietors now crisping languid
under Florida sun. And flap-jowled Mayor Daley,
our big benevolent murderous daddy,
gifted us with high-rise castles crafted of dirty dollars,
battered cans of bumpy milk, free cheese.

To know Gwen, you need to know the Alex,
the only movie theater West, where frisky rats
big as toddlers poked slow noses into your popcorn,
then locked red round eyes on Cleopatra Jones
and sat, confident and transfixed.

After the movies and any street corner's fried lunch,
we'd head to "the store in back of that fat man's house"
to surrender hoarded quarters for the latest 45,
stripped licorice in black or red,
pork rinds, Boston Baked Beans,
or fat sour pickles floating in a jar in the corner.
The fat man's wife, Miss Caroline,
plunged her hammy forearm into the brine,
pulled out the exact pickle you pointed to
and shoved it deep into a single-ply paper bag.
Only the truly Negro would then poke
a peppermint stick down the center of that pickle
and slurp the dizzy of salt and sugar.
We gnawed rock-stiff candy dots off paper columns,
suffered Lemonheads and Red Hots,
pushed neon sweatsocks down on Vaselined calves,
and my Lord, we learned to switch. For a dime,
the fat man would warm up the record player,
click reject and give us a hit of Ms. Fontella Bass's
heartbroke heart clamoring for rescue,
or Ruby Andrews steady wailing in a woman way.

There were so many millions of each one of us,
ashy goddesses walking the wild West,
strutting past sloped storefronts where brown meat
and hog heads crowded the windows,
past shuttered groceries, and gas stations
with pump boys eyeing our new undulating asses,
past fashion palaces where almost no money

satisfied our yearning for hollow glamour
with cheap threads already unraveling.

Observe the kick-ass angle of our crowns.
Chicago girls just keep coming back.
They don't hear you,
they don't see you,
they ain't never really needed you.
They got the Holy Ghost and Garfield Park,
on one city block, they got a hundred ways to buy chicken,
they jump rope nasty and barefoot in the dirt,
they got the *ooh achie koo,*
the pink plastic clothesline underhand,
they got the slip bone. They got the Gwen in them.

Any jazz could be ours, and her jazz was.
Unflinching in riotous headwrap
and thick, two-shades-too stockings,
she penned the soundtrack of we because she knew,
because she was skinny early church and not bending,
because no man could ever hold her the way hurt did,
because she could peer at you over those Coke-bottle specs,
fast gal, and turn the sorry sight of you into her next poem.

Each year she stays gone, we colored girls aimlessly bop
and search dangerous places for music.
Chicago bows its huge head, grudgingly accepts spring.

God, if there is a You, there must surely still be a her.
Stop the relentless seasons. Show us Your face,
explain Your skewed timing,
Your wacky choice of angels.

13 WAYS OF LOOKING AT 13

[handwritten: Starting her cycle]

I.

You touch your forefinger to the fat clots in the blood,
then lift its iron stench to look close, searching the globs
of black scarlet for the dimming swirl of dead children.
You thread one thick pad's cottony tail, then the other,
through the little steel guides of the belt. You stand and lift
the contraption, press your thighs close to adjust the bulk,
then bend to pull up coarse white cotton panties bleached blue,
and just to be safe, you pin the bottom of the pad
to the shredding crotch of the Carter's. And then you spritz
the guilty air with the cloying kiss of FDS. *[handwritten: → air freshner?]*
It's time to begin the game of justifying ache,
time to name the mystery prickling that's riding your skin.
You're convinced the boys can smell you, and they can, they can.

[handwritten: She was self conscious / embarrassed]

2.

Right now, this Tuesday in July, nothing's headier *[handwritten: trying to make her hair like this]*
than the words *Sheen! Manageable! Bounce!* Squinting into
the smeared mirror, you search your ghetto-ripe head for them,
you probe with greased fingers, spreading paths in the chaos
wide enough for the advertised glimmer to escape,
but your snarls hold tight to their woven dry confounding.
Fevered strands snap under the drag of the wiry brush
and order unfurls, while down the hall Mama rotates
the hot comb in a bleary blaze, smacks her joyful gum.
Still, TV bellows its promise. You witness the pink
snap of the perfect neck, hear the impossible vow—
Shampoo with this! *Sheen! Bounce!* Her cornsilk head is gospel,
it's true. *C'mon chile!* Even Mama's summoning burns.

[handwritten: getting her hair straightening by a hot womb (really torture, but necessary for beauty)]

[handwritten: tied to the Bluest Eye's vision of beauty]

72

3.

Ms. Stein scribbled a word on the blackboard, said *Who can*
pronounce this? and the word was *anemone* and from
that moment you first felt the clutter of possible
in your mouth, from the time you stumbled through the rhythm
and she slow-smiled, you suddenly knew you had the right
to be explosive, to sling syllables through back doors,
to make up your own damned words just when you needed them.
All that day, sweet *anemone* tangled in your teeth,
spurted sugar tongue, led you to the dictionary
where you were assured that it existed, to the cave
of the bathroom where you warbled it in bounce echo,
and, finally convinced you owned that teeny gospel,
you wrote it again and again and again and a—.

4.

Trying hard to turn hips to slivers, sway to stutter,
you walk past the Sinclair station where lanky boys, dust
in their hair, dressed in their uniforms of oil and thud,
rename you *pussy* with their eyes. They bring sounds shudder
and blue from their throats just for you, serve up the ancient
sonata of skin drum and conch shell, sing suggesting woos
of AM radio, boom, boom, *How you gon' just walk*
on by like that? and suddenly you know why you are
stitched so tight, crammed like a flash bomb into pinafore,
obeying Mama's instructions to be a baby
as long as you can. Because it's a man's world and James
Brown is gasoline, the other side of slow zippers.
He is all of it, the pump, pump, the growled *please please please.*

5.

You try to keep your hands off your face, but the white-capped
pimples might harbor evil. It looks like something cursed
is trying to escape your cheeks, your whole soul could be
involved. So you pinch, squeeze, and pop, let the smelly snow
splash the mirror, slather your fresh-scarred landscape with creams
that clog and strangle. At night, you look just like someone
obsessed with the moon, its gruff superstitions, its lies.
Your skin is a patchwork of wishing. You scrub and dab
and mask and surround, you bombard, spritz, and peel, rubbing
alcohol, flesh-toned Clearasil that pinkens and cakes
while new dirtworms shimmy beneath the pummeled surface
of you. Every time you touch your face, you leave a scar.
Hey, you. Every time you touch your face, you leave a scar.

6.

You want it all: chicken wings with bubbled skin fried tight,
salmon cakes in syrup, the most improbable parts
of swine, oily sardines on saltines splashed in red spark,
chitlins nurtured and scraped in Saturday assembly,
buttered piecrusts stuffed with sweet potatoes and sugar,
gray cheese conjured from the heads of hogs. All that Dixie
dirt binds, punches your insides flat, reteaches the blind
beat of your days. Like Mama and her mother before
her, you pulse on what is thrown away—gray hog guts stewed
improbable and limp, scrawny chicken necks merely
whispering meat. You will live beyond the naysayers,
your rebellious heart constructed of lard and salt, your
life labored but long. You are built of what should kill you.

7.

Always treat white folks right, your mama's mantra again
and yet again, *because they give you things.* Like credit,
compliments, passing grades, government jobs, direction,
extra S&H stamps, produce painted to look fresh,
a religion. When the insurance man came, she snapped
herself alive, hurriedly rearranged her warm bulk. He
was balding badly, thatches of brown on a scabbed globe.
Just sign here, he hissed, staring crave into her huge breasts,
pocketing the death cash, money she would pay and pay
and never see again. *C'mere girl, say hello to*
Mister Fred. She had taught you to bow. She taught him
to ignore the gesture, to lock his watering eyes
to yours and lick his dry lips with a thick, coated tongue.

reminded me of Mr. Henry being creepy

8.

In the bathroom of the what-not joint on the way to
school, you get rid of the starch and billowed lace, barrettes
taming unraveling braids, white kneesocks and sensible
hues. From a plastic bag, you take out electric blue
eye shadow, platforms with silver-glittered heels, neon
fishnets, and a blouse that doesn't so much button as
snap shut. The transformation takes five minutes, and you
emerge feeling like a budding lady but looking,
in retrospect, like a blind streetwalker bursting from
a cocoon. This is what television does, turns your
mother into clueless backdrop, fills your pressed head with
the probability of thrum. Your body becomes
just not yours anymore. It's a dumb little marquee.

trying to become like a lady

aung aing rewing up

— transformation —

75

9.

With your bedroom door closed, you are skyscraper bouffant,
peach foundation, eyelashes like upturned claws. You are
exuding ice, pinched all over by earrings, you are
way too much woman for this room. The audience has
one chest, a single shared chance to gasp. They shudder, heave,
waiting for you to open your mouth and break their hearts.
Taking the stage, you become an S, pour ache into your
hip swings, *tsk tsk* as the front row collapses. Damn, they
want you. You lift the microphone, something illegal
comes out of you, a sound like titties and oil. Mama
flings the door open with a church version of your name.
Then you are pimpled, sexless, ashed and doubledutch knees.
You are spindles. You are singing into a hairbrush.

10.

This is what everyone else is doing: skating in
soul circles, skinning shins, tongue-kissing in the coatroom,
skimming alleys for Chicago rats, failing English, math,
crushing curfew, lying about yesterday and age,
slipping Woolworth's bounty into an inside pocket,
sprouting breasts. Here is what everyone else is doing:
sampling the hotness of hootch, grinding under blue light,
getting turned around in the subway, flinging all them
curse words, inhaling a quick supper before supper
fried up in hot Crisco and granulated sugar,
sneaking out through open windows when the night goes dark,
calling mamas bitches under their breath, staying up
till dawn to see what hides. What *you* are doing: Reading.

11.

your role at age of 13 (Bluest Eye similarity)

You are never too old. And you are never too world,
too almost grown, you are never correct, no matter
how many times you are corrected. It is never
too late, never too early to be told to cross the
street to the place where the wild stuff is, to suffer her
instructions: *No, not that little switch, get the big one,*
the one that makes that good whipping sound when the breeze blows,
and you are never too fast crossing the boulevard
to bring it back while winged sedans carve jazz on your path.
You climb the stairs, she screams *Get up here!* The door to where
you live with her flies open. She snatches the thorned branch,
whips it a hundred times across the backs of your legs.
You want her to die. Not once, no. Many times. Gently.

12.

skin tone

That boy does not see you. He sees through you, past your tone
of undecided earth. You are the exact shade of
the failed paper bag test, the Aunt Esther, you are hair
forever turning back in the direction from which
it came. You are clacking knees and nails bitten to blood.
Stumbling forth in black, Jesus-prescribed shoes, you have no
knowledge of his knowledge of hip sling and thrust. That boy
does not see you. So squeeze your eyes shut and imagine
your mouth touching the swell of his forearm. Imagine
just your name's first syllable in the sugared well of
his throat. Dream of all the ways he is not walking past
you again, turning his eyes to the place where you are,
where you're standing, where you shake, where you pray, where you aren't.

darker man ... paper bag

strong, black woman (can be angry and abuse black men)

Aunt Esther is not supposed to be beautiful or something desirable, a turn of for a 13 year old girl

13.
You're almost fourteen. And you think you're ready to push
beyond the brutal wisdoms of the one and the three,
but some nagging crave in you doesn't want to let go.
You suspect that you will never be this unfinished,
all Hail Mary and precipice, stuttering sashay,
fuses in your swollen chest suddenly lit, spitting,
and you'll need to give your hips a name for what they did
while you weren't there. You'll miss the pervasive fever that
signals bloom, the sore lessons of jumprope in your calves.
This is the last year your father is allowed to touch
you. Sighing, you push Barbie's perfect body through the
thick dust of a top shelf. There her prideful heart thunders.
She has hardened you well. She has taught you everything.

[handwritten annotations:]
? not rape, innocently
finally growing up
Bluest Eye / baby doll
societies way of how you're supposed to look
(not throwing it away tho)

78

DEAR JIMMY CONNOLL

Dear Jimmy Connoll, who snatched an ill-fitting but culturally snug Afro wig from my head while I stood in the chow line on a Tuesday at roughly 12:30 p.m. at Carl Schurz High School on the northwest side of Chi: O.K., maybe you suspected that it was just a weirdness plopped atop me, you couldn't have known that the damn thing wasn't anchored down by bobby pins or that my real hair was flat plaited dusty and matted beneath because that Tuesday all I cared about was the sheen that showed, not the shameful itch beneath. The stated color of the wig, Jet Black 1A, was actually two shades too black for me, just some cheap tangle meant to imitate real hair 'cause real hair cost up in the dollars and I was just stalking the kink anyway, the natural ignored root. Didn't want to rattle anyone.

Dear Jimmy, I was your public personal curiosity, mantel-ready and scrub-skinned in your presence, aching through the ritual of Tri-Hi-Y and Latin Club, every word I spoke tilted obediently *up* at the *end*. I was a thing with no color. But it was 1970, a year with its stupid fist in the air, and since my hair was the only thing I couldn't change (yes, I still believed that pesky skin thing could be negotiated), I surrendered to letting those naps say Negro out loud. There it was, undeniable, shifting as I stumbled, the front inching down my forehead, the back lifting for a flash of private knotting, oh no, I was way too big a slice of colored, something had to be done. Jimmy, how noble of you to take it upon yourself, to slap me back to center, to staunch my wacky revolution. What courage it took for you to confront that most formidable wrong.

Remember when you held me in your arms? You were chaperone at a freshman dance, and by then I was so in love with you my ribs ached from struggling to hold that huge sin in. A downbeat,

you with arms outstretched, and I signed myself over, told myself
maybe he, maybe I, dared a *maybe we,* prayed me pale and pliant,
prayed you'd wash me woman with that stabbing blue Jesus gaze.
When the music stopped, your mouth touched my cheek, and I
dizzied myself writing, dreaming, building whole futures on that
blazing square of skin. Now I know you were aping the room over
my shoulder, googoo jungle mug, *look at me rocking the world
of the colored girl!* Later I bet you laughed, mocked how my hips
sought yours, bubbled your perfect lips obscenely, hooted monkey.

Dear Jimmy Connoll, did you talk about it with your friends, did you
snicker and plan, did you think about the second after, whether you
would drop the wig at my feet or run away holding it high over your
head? You held it out and I took it. And all my air became pointing
fingers, open mouths, shouts from the windows, laughing from
the floorboards, guffaws from the wiry crown uncurling in my hand.
You stood your ground, smiled sweet simply, urged me to understand.
I looked numbly at the thing that I held. Suddenly I was blacker than
I ever was, colored all over everything, Negro was unleashed, jigaboo
came tumbling down, jungle bunny came out of hiding. My real hair
unflattened in new air, popped its day of dust and sprang corkscrews,
lending the drama its only motion. I opened my mouth to drown you
in raging, rip deep gash through the god of you. But all that came out,
stunned for all this time, were the first three words of this poem.

CARNIE

Not good enough, not teeth enough, for Riverview,
he rolls into town under the shoulders of night with
his sleazed and pimpled caravan. Taught to screech
inwardly at his filth, we nevertheless find ourselves
drawn to his gray devastation of grin, the sneaky way
stories map themselves onto the backs of his hands.
Girls, giddy in the throes of repulsion, can't help
visioning him as a blazing and wordless fuck, skin
sandy, grating, the mud of his open mouth sliding all
over us. His snake-lidded eyes know how we resent
balance. In line, steamed and bewildered, we consider
his bitter knowledge of levers and gears, listen to
muttered instructions on all the best ways not to die.
And admit it now, little girl. With spit and the heel
of a hand, you seek to be wildly industrious. You
want to clean off a place on his body, find a patch
of landscape the sun has not quite killed, and you
want to wallow in the dirt denied you by Mama,
screaming into the blue of freefall, riding the natural
stink off that boy. And you got your head thrown back.

GUESS WHO'S CLOSEST TO HEAVEN

Forefinger, nail clipped blunt, breaks the chill skin
of the pomade, tunnels for the bottom
of the tin, scoops out a sweet-scented lump.
Smeared between slow hands, the smell breaks open,
life leaking from violet, and lends Sunday
stink to thin hair wired and dark from washing.

And this happens behind so many doors—
in Mister Odell's cluttered kitchenette,
in Freddy the butcher's misted mirror.
They groom for glory, snap on dull Spiedels,
pour all of their ache into squarish serge.
They are so close to dying they can tell
you what their heaven smells like and it smells
different for each of them: to Mister Earl,
it's steam and anise. To Ole James Markum,
dead-slow knotting his noose of a necktie,
heaven smells of Tuscaloosa summer.

Between them and there, perhaps another
hundred Sundays of can't-flinch ritual,
splashing pungent scent into throat hollows
and cave of the chest, treating tired wingtips
to a Vaseline shimmer. Old suits freed
from plastic, creases blade-sharp, double-checked.

And then on Sunday, Second Street Baptist
or Pilgrim Rest Missionary Baptist
or Church of the Living Lord opens up
before them with its splintered pews and fat,

peach-powdered usherettes. Our men rock with
The Word, feel that huge holy hand icing
their spines. Content with being softly doomed,
they mumble memorized gospel and feel
a hollow swell inside them. They pray for

minor comforts, their knees hurting like hell
with the coming thunder. But no amount
of kneeling can move those suits. And, goddamn.

Their hair is perfect.

HIS FOR THE TAKING

My mother's sister, Mary Sanders, wailed
You muthafucka! just before throat-snorting
the contents of her perfectly-portioned dinner
and hawking a glob of it toward the wall
beside my head. Her eyes were rolling worlds,
lit maniacally from behind, her hair steamed
and untwirling. The hospital room smelled
warmly of spittle, scream, and scrubbed piss,
and again I cursed my mother for portioning
my teenage time this way, charging me with
the third-shift-weekends spoon-feeding of my
unraveled aunt, her brain dimmed and distanced
by Alzheimer's and errant shards of Mississippi.

She recognized none of us, slapped and spat
at our attempts to be relatives, and reveled
in her new hot vocabulary, rolling *goddamnit*
and *shit* and *kiss my black country ass* around
on her formerly God-fearing Delta tongue.
I pressed buttons for her, inched forkfuls
of dry chicken toward her clenched teeth,
wiped her venom from my cheeks and hair.
Other sicknesses whistled through her pores
and she slept fitfully, feces drying under her nails.

It was weeks before I noticed that my mother
wasn't part of the reluctant rotation of caregivers.
She spent her days just outside the closed door
of her sister's dismantling, numb to the blaring,
praying for God to enter the hospital room,
wrap His tired arms around someone, and leave.

DIRTY DIANA

There are oh-so-many things a woman can do with the business
end of a diamond. Cut a man's throat and the blood rinses away
easily. Slice an eerie, convincing grin into the back of your head.
Gut a rival. Snip an emergency hem to release the utter glamour
of knobbed knees. Magically turn Tuesday's wig into Saturday's.
The secret is to never stop crooning, to inject your roundabout lyric
with air, a little violence, frosted water. Warble like you were born
with the engine of switched hips, like your breasts suddenly swing
beyond your absence of breasts. Ms. Ross, you will be underestimated.
Just make sure they never find out how you killed Florence, slyly
slipping just the slightest hesitation into her fat heart, introducing
the suggestion that it explode. Fling glitter at their faces and cup
a diamond in your palm. Shimmy your history into a sequined
sheath, where no one will ever find it. Disguise it as sin, as sway.

AN OPEN LETTER TO JOSEPH PETER NARAS

or, The Regrettable Dramatic Arc of Loving a White Boy

It's a wonder our grind never toppled, that we were lap and gulp sincerely, lips layered away, pubics in expecting parallel, burning the outlawed outline of our writhe into the lawn, outlandish hues vital and nasty in erupting weeds, our bound structure never wearying of the questioning prod, the wishful pummel, ninth period over, the snarlers and spitters slow gone and we were out loud, right out in the open, out of our damned minds running our tongues around the edges of war, how socially insane our primal twist, the doomed conjoined clock of us, the engine of our against, your fingers a disruption in hair just learning to explode. Every Thursday, Tuesday, Friday, Monday, Wednesday, we stumbled in frustrated dangle away from the grounds of Carl Schurz High School, temperatures skewered, our souths hammered and drip through denims. Separate buses spit their oily smoke to the north and west and we pressed radiant genital ache into the ride, red-inking continued crave into matching notebooks, our poetry ripped through with dactyls and something no one but two ballad-battered fools would call a future.

Love at *our* sixteen smothered the jointly-addressed niggernote.

Don't know

why it took your father's friend so long to see us, to witness our open wounds browning the grass. Imagine his gape his flushed *goddamnit* his bulge-eyed conviction to upright the collapsing, to shove the wild wayward back into orbit, to push those colors back inside the lines, to reteach the day away from the fall. I've dreamed often of his vile and sputtered reportage, spittle showering the receiver, every other word a resolute and hurtled scarlet.

AN OPEN LETTER TO JOSEPH PETER NARAS, TAKE 2

or, Today's After-School Special Veers into Explosive Territory

Let me tell you why it never occurred to me to be afraid.

You took off your glasses, and you were perfect, eyes bluer
than any prince written, reachably gorgeous, no hiccup
of light when you stretched for me. No discussion of why
we shouldn't tangle and pump against your locker between
periods, why I shouldn't wrap yards of yarn around your
class ring, wear it dripped between new breasts. We snuck
around and about and pretended normal, lying to parents
about meetings and committees, entering the junior prom
through separate doors, boy, damn decorum, I loved you.
I know I did because I know some things by now. I know
that your body was a wizened and ill advised battlefield
against mine, that your mouth was razored, that "I love you"
was a huge and unwieldy declaration, the kind of blue you
immediately unforgive. My parents weren't yours. They
considered you the naptime-sized American dream, a rung
on the stepladder, the climb every white-capped mountain.
Just be careful, they said, while your father spat blades, said
(these are the words I've imagined, slapped with the wide-eye)
*I'll throw you out of my house if I hear about you seeing
that black girl again.* Joe, I loved you then, and I love you
still. We are drama born of the truth tell, our tongues so stupid
and urged they continually reached the back of our throats.
Who hates me for actually knowing this? There are hundreds
of songs written about all the things you can't do at sixteen.
There are a million songs written about what I didn't do with you.

5

WAIT

AN OPEN LETTER TO JOSEPH PETER NARAS, TAKE 3

or, Cue the Waterworks

When I was a kid, my mother convinced my father that I'd done
something terrible, she urged him to spank me, and he did.
His blows were reluctant pillows, pullback and whisper slow,
more for appearance than correction, and while he whupped,
he cried. Slow, beautiful cries, elegant and silent, he wept.
After vowing to never touch his daughter that way, he went
through the prescribed motions, hiding his tears, and I bucked,
bellowed, scripting my twist, knowing what drama was required.
That was the first time I saw a man cry. When your dad became
a bomb, vowing to blow at the continued thought of your mouth
on me, we stood at the bus stop that last day, matching fingertips,
major players in a terrible love story's climactic scene. I boarded
the bus and clawed the window while you stood on the sidewalk,
the sugar of what we'd been staining your cheeks; all that was
missing were the drooped tulips and aching strings. And the gulp
that happens when a man loses hold and forgets the definition
of man. I wonder if your father ever wonders where I am.
I wonder if he wonders who I was.

ASKING FOR A HEART ATTACK

For Aretha Franklin

Aretha. Deep butter dipped, scorched pot liquor,
swift lick off the sugar cane. Vaselined knees
clack gospel, hinder the waddling South. 'Retha.
Greased, she glows in limelit circle, defending
her presence with a sanctified moan, ass rumbling
toward curfew's backstreets where jukes still gulp silver.

Goddess of Hoppin' John and bumped buttermilk,
girl know Jesus by His *first* name. She the one
sang His drooping down from ragged wooden т,
dressed Him in blood-red shine, conked that holy head,
rustled up excuses for bus fare and took
the Deity downtown. They found a neon
backslap, coaxed the DJ and slid electric
till the lights slammed on. *Don't know where you goin',
who you going with, but you sho can't stay here.*

Aretha taught the Good Son slow, dirty
words for His daddy's handiwork, laughed as he
first sniffed whiskey's surface, hissed him away when
he sought to touch His hand to the blue in her.
She was young then, spindly and thin ribs paining,
her heartbox thrumming in a suspicious key.
So Jesus blessed her, opened her throat and taught
her to *wail that way she do, Lawd she do wail
that way don't she do that wail the way she do
wail that way, don't she? That girl can wail that way.*
Now when Aretha's fleeing screech jump from juke

and reach been-done-wrong bone, all the Lord can do
is stand at a wary distance and applaud.
Oh yeah, and maybe shield His heart a little.

So you question her several shoulders,
the soft stairs of flesh leading to her chins,
the steel bones of an impossible dress
gnawing raw into bubbling obliques?

Ain't your mama never schooled you in how
black women collect the world, build other
bodies onto our own? No earthly man
knows the solution to our hips, asses
urgent as sirens, our titties bursting
with traveled roads. Ask Aretha just what
Jesus whispered to her that night about
the gospel hidden in lard and sugar.
She'll tell you why black girls grow fat
away from the world, and toward each other.

HIP-HOP GHAZAL

Gotta love us brown girls, munching on fat, swinging blue hips,
decked out in shells and splashes, Lawdie, bringing them woo hips.

As the jukebox teases, watch my sistas throat the heartbreak,
inhaling bass line, cracking backbone and singing thru hips.

Like something boneless, we glide silent, seeping 'tween floorboards,
wrapping around the hims, and *ooh wee,* clinging like glue hips.

Engines, grinding, rotating, smokin', gotta pull back some.
Natural minds are lost at the mere sight of swinging true hips.

Gotta love us girls, just struttin' down Chicago streets
killing the menfolk with a dose of that stinging view. Hips.

Crying 'bout getting old—Patricia, you need to get up off
what God gave you. Say a prayer and start slinging. Cue hips.

LOOKING TO SEE HOW THE EYES INHABIT DARK, WONDERING ABOUT LIGHT

In December 1999, Stevie Wonder sought to undergo an operation to partially restore his sight. He made the round of talk shows, trumpeting the possibilities, before the story dropped off the radar. Doctors had declared that he was not a good candidate for the procedure.

Look. When he assumes he is alone, he absently claws the air for light.
See how he pulls the sun toward himself. Even as he conjures, wonders,
eyes spit their cruel blanks, drench him in mud. His mama is the dark;
dark is his daddy. A shiver in his lids becomes his next church, his eyes
wonder at the black bottomless flash, the siphoning of narrative. He can see
light as it exists in memory—lush, fleeting, then maddening. *Made ya look.*

Darkness strives to be his comfort. But he is obsessed by the need to look,
eyes flat, roiling, his head adjusting *as if.* He tilts toward each tongue of light,
wonders at its evil sweet, squints, strains. Dark whispers, *if you must see,*
see the gifts I have given—the unflinching knowledge of self, the wild wonder
light has birthed in you, how it blooms without answer. He touches his eye.
Look. He lifts the lid, pokes the dead orb with a finger, cries out again to dark.

Seasons change only on his skin. Chill and steam nudge the edges of dark.
Wondering what year, what June, what clock it is, his useless eyes look,
light upon layered shadow, scan the unraveled empty. He curses those eyes,
eyes that simply loll and water and grow impossibly wide, clawing for light.
Look how completely he has learned the language of the hand, stark wonder
darkening weary palms as he presses them flat against against, wanting to see.

Eyes, they say, can be sexed, propped wide, flooded with daybreak. He'll see
lightning, dim dance, maybe a minute of day. Doctors tout the shattered dark,
look beneath trembling lids for doors, promise his child's face. And he wonders—

wonder being the only response he trusts—as hope is unleashed. It hurts to look.
Dark, desperately clutching, woos him, redefines beauty as the absence of light.
See his torso ripple, how he fights with his own fingers, how he weeps for eyes.

Wonder how long it will take before those who whisper the promise of eyes
look hard at the one-soul religion they've crafted, scan their data and finally see
dark as it owns him—numb to their screeching miracles, overpowering the light?
Light is overrated, they decide. Best not to shock the system, rip holes in the dark,
see up close the cacophonous stanzas sight scribbles over time. It hurts to look.
Eyes overwork, tangle lessons best learned by touch. It's much safer to wonder.

Light a match, wave it back and forth, watch him follow the waltzing heat. Wonder,
darkly, what hollow blessings he has left to cling to. He follows music with his eyes,
sees the notes rollick black upon black. He snakes his balding head, pretends to look,
looking like a man who has never watched another man move. Now it's easy to see—
eyes would ruin him. Shadow puppets have answered every question. The dark,
wonderful, forgiving, takes his hand and leads him, like a lover, away from the light.

Light simply makes us wonder and crave the dark.
I've seen how desperately you look for me.

THIEF OF TONGUES

[handwritten: if you want to be respected, you have to speak like it]

I.

My mother is learning English.
Pulling rubbery cinnamon-tinged hose to a roll beneath
her knees, sporting one swirling Baptist ski slope of a hat,
she rides the rattling elevated to a Windy City spire
and pulls back her gulp as the elevator hurtles heaven.
Then she's stiffly seated at a scarred oak table
across from a white, government-sanctioned savior
who has dedicated eight hours a week to straightening
afflicted black tongues. She guides my mother
patiently through lazy *ings* and *ers,* slowly scraping
her throat clean of the moist and raging infection
of Aliceville, Alabama. There are barely muttered
apologies for colored sounds. There is much beginning again.

I want to talk right before I die.
Want to stop saying "ain't" and "I done been"
like I ain't got no sense. I'm a grown woman.
I done lived too long to be stupid,
acting like I just got off the boat.

[handwritten: what the mother thinks?]

My mother
has never been
on a boat.

But fifty years ago, merely a million of her,
clutching strapped cases, *Jet*'s Emmett Till issue,
and thick-peppered chicken wings in waxed bags,
stepped off hot rumbling buses at Northern depots
in Detroit, in Philly, in the bricked cornfield of Chicago.

Brushing stubborn scarlet dust from their shoes,
they said *We North now,* slinging it in backdoor syllable,
as if those three words were vessels big enough
to hold country folks' overwrought ideas of light.

2.

Back then, my mother thought it a modern miracle,
this new living in a box stacked upon other boxes,
where every flat surface reeked of Lysol and effort,
and chubby roaches, cross-eyed with Raid,
dragged themselves across freshly washed dishes
and dropped dizzy from the ceiling into our Murphy beds,
our washtubs, our open steaming pots of collards.

very far

Of course, there was a factory just two bus rides close,
a job that didn't involve white babies or bluing laundry,
where she worked in tense line with other dreamers: *anxious?*
Repeatedly. Repeatedly. Repeatedly. Repeatedly,
all those oily hotcombed heads drooping, no talking   *imperfect hands*
as scarred brown hands romanced machines, just   *make the*
the sound of doin' it right, and Juicy Fruit crackling.   *machines work perfectly*
A mere mindset away, there had to be a corner tavern
where dead bluesmen begged second chances from the juke,
and where my mama, perched man-wary on a comfortable stool
by the door, could look like a Christian who was just leaving.

refers to the move to the north

And on Sunday, at Pilgrim Rest Missionary Baptist Church,
she would pull on the pure white gloves of service   *← sunday's best outfit for*
and wail to the rafters when the Holy Ghost's hot hand   *mass (southern life)*
grew itchy and insistent at the small of her back.
She was His child, finally loosed of that damnable Delta,
building herself anew in this land of sidewalks,   *would be an usher (white glove)*
blue jukes, and sizzling fried perch in virgin-white boxes.

this is a step to get to the dream

elements of southern life

speaking in tongues

Religions

not over-minking the language

could be letting her anger out

98

geographical area

See her: all nap burned from her crown, one gold tooth
winking, soft hair riding her lip, blouses starched hard,
orlon sweaters with smatterings of stitched roses,
A-line skirts the color of <u>unleashed winter.</u>

3.   *southern*

My mother's voice is like <u>homemade cornbread,</u>
slathered with butter, full of places for <u>heat to hide.</u> *usually think of*
When she is pissed, it punches straight out   *cornbread as sweet*
and clears the room. When she is scared,
it turns practical, matter-of-fact, like when she called
to say
They found your daddy this morning,
somebody shot him, he dead.
He ain't come to work this morning, I knowed
something was wrong.
When mama talks, the Southern swing of it
is wild with unexpected blooms, *does she regret leaving?*
like the fields she never told me about in Alabama. → *Hiding/ escaping/*
Her rap is peppered with *ain't gots* and *I done beens* *avoiding her past*
and *he be's* just like mine is when I'm color among color.
During worship, when <u>talk becomes song,</u> her voice collapses ↓
and loses all acquaintance with key, so of course,   *incorrectly*
                          broken- bad english (broken english)
it's my mother's <u>fractured</u> alto wailing above everyone—
[uncaged, unapologetic and creaking toward heaven.] *HER WAILING*
          can't fake this- it
              breaks down
Now she <u>wants to sound proper</u> when she gets there.
A woman got some sense and future need to upright herself,
talk English instead of talking wrong.

It's strange to hear the precise rote of Annie Pearl's new mouth.
She slips sometimes, but is proud when she remembers
to bite down on dirt-crafted contractions and double negatives.

Sometimes I wonder whatever happened to the warm expanse
of the red-dust woman, who arrived with a little sin
and all the good wrong words. I dream her breathless,
maybe leaning forward a little in her seat on the Greyhound.
I ain't never seen, she begins, grinning through the grime
at Chicago, city of huge shoulders, thief of tongues.

where did her mom go—new language makes her seem like a new person

MOTOWN CROWN

The Temps, all swerve and pivot, conjured schemes
that had us skipping school, made us forget
how mamas schooled us hard against the threat
of five-part harmony and sharkskin seams.
We spent our school days balanced on the beams
of moon we wished upon, the needled jet-
black 45s that spun and hadn't yet
become the dizzy spinning of our dreams.
Sugar Pie, Honey Bunch . . . oh, you
loved our tangled hair and rusty knees.
Marvin Gaye slowed down while we gave chase
then wowed us with his skinny hips, on cue.
We hungered for the anguished screech of *Please*
from soulful throats. Relentless. Booming bass.

From soulful throats, relentless booming bass
softened with the turn of Smokey's key.
His languid, liquid, luscious, aching plea
for bodies we didn't have yet made a case
for lying to ourselves. He would embrace
our naps and raging pimples. We could see
his croon inside our clothes. His pedigree
of milky flawless skin meant we'd replace
our *daddies* with his fine and lanky frame.
I did you wrong, my heart went out to play
he serenaded, filling up the space
that separated Smoke from certain flame.
Couldn't comprehend the drug of him, his sway,
silk where his throat should be. He growled such grace.

Silk where his throat should be, and growling grace,
Little Stevie made us wonder why
we even *needed* sight. His rhythm eye
could see us click our hips and pump in place
whenever he cut loose. Ooh, we'd unlace
our Converse All-Stars, yeah, we wondered why
we couldn't get down *without* our shoes. We'd try
to dance and keep up with his funky pace
of hiss and howl and hum, and then he'd slow
to twist our hearts until he heard them crack,
ignoring lonesome leaking from the seams.
The rockin' blind boy couldn't help but show
us light. We wailed his every soulful track
through open windows, 'neath the door—pipe dreams.

Through open windows, 'neath the doors, pipe dreams
served up bone, bouffant, the serpentine
and bug-eyed Lady D, the boisterous queen
of overdone, her body built from beams
of awkward light. Her slithering extremes
just made us feel so small. Insanely lean,
everywhere she stepped she caused a scene.
We craved her wigs and waist and crafted schemes
that would insure our hips would soon be thin,
that we'd hear symphonies, wouldn't hurry love,
cause Diana said *Make sure it gleams*
no matter what it is. Her different spin,
a voice like sugar air, no inkling of
a soul beneath the vinyl. The Supremes.

That soul beneath the vinyl, the Supremes
knew nothing of it. They were breathy sighs
and flowing hips, soul music's booby prize.
But Mary Wells, so drained of self-esteem,
was a pudgy, barstool-ridin' bucktoothed dream
who none of us would dare to idolize
out loud. She had our nightmares memorized
and like or like it not, she wailed our theme
while her too-blackness made us ill at ease
and we smeared Artra on to reach for white.
When Mary's *My Guy* blared, we didn't think race,
cause there was all that romance, and the keys
that Motown held. Unlocked, we'd soon ignite.
We stockpiled extra sequins, just in case.

We stockpiled extra sequins, just in case
the Marvelettes pronounced we'd benefit
from little dabs of shine. If we could get
inside their swirl, a kinda naughty place,
we knew that all the boys would have to brace
themselves against our heat, much too legit
to dress up as some other thing. We split
our blue jeans trying to match their pace.
And soon our breasts began to pop, we spoke
in bluer tones, and Berry Gordy looked
and licked his lips. Our only saving grace?
The luscious, liquid languid tone of Smoke,
the soundtrack while our A-cup bras unhooked.
Our sudden Negro hips required more space.

Our sudden Negro hips required more space,
but we pretended not to feel that spill
that changed the way we walked. And yes, we still
felt nappy, awkward, strangely out of place
while Motown crammed our eager hearts with lace
and storylines. Romance was all uphill.
No push, no prod, no bitter magic pill
could lift us to its light. And not a trace
of prizes they said we'd already won.
As mamas called on Jesus, shook their heads
and mourned our Delta names, we didn't deem
to care. Religion—there was only one.
We took transistor preachers to our beds
and Smokey sang a lyric dripping cream.

While Smokey sang a lyric dripping cream,
Levi tried to woo us with his growl:
Can't help myself. Admitted with a scowl,
this bit of weakness was a clever scheme
to keep us screaming, front row, under gleam
of lights, beside the speakers' blasting vowels.
We rocked and steamed. Levi, on the prowl,
glowed black, a savior in the stage light's beam.
But then the stage light dimmed, and there we were
in bodies primed—for what we didn't know.
We sang off-key while skipping home alone.
Deceptions that you sing to tend to blur
and disappear in dance, why is that so?
Ask any colored girl and she will moan.

Ask any colored girl and she will moan
an answer with a downbeat and a sleek
five-part croon. She's dazzled, and she'll shriek
what she's been taught. She won't long be alone,
or crazed with wanting more. One day she'll own
that quiet heart that Motown taught to speak,
she'll know that being the same makes her unique.
She'll worship at the god of microphone
until the bass line booms, until some old
Temptation leers and says *I'll take you home
and heal you in the way the music vowed.*
She's mesmerized—his moves, his tooth is gold.
She dances to the drumbeat of his poem,
remembering how. Love had lied so loud.

Remembering how love had lied so loud,
we tangled in the rhythms that we chose.
Seduced by thump and sequins, heaven knows
we tried to live our hopeful lives unbowed,
but bending led to break. We were so proud
to mirror every lyric. Radios
spit beg and mend, and sturdy stereos
told us what we were and weren't allowed.
Our daddies sweat in factories while we
found other daddies under limelight's glow.
Desperate, we begged them to illuminate
the glitter lives they said they'd guarantee
would save us. But instead, the crippling blow.
We whimpered while the downbeat dangled bait.

We whimpered while the downbeat dangled bait,
we leapt and swallowed all the music said
while Smokey laughed and Marvin fell and bled.
Their sinning slapped us hard and slapped us straight,
and even then, we listened for the great
announcement of the drum, for tune to spread,
a Marvelette to pick up on the thread.
But as we know by now, it's much too late
to reconsider love, or claw our way
through all the glow they tossed to slow our roll.
What we know now we should have always known.
When Smokey winked at us and whispered *They
don't love you like I do,* he snagged our soul.
We wound up doing the slow drag, all alone.

They made us do the slow drag, all alone.
They made us kiss our mirrors, deal with heat
and hips we couldn't control. They danced deceit
and we did too, addicted to the drone
of revelation and the verses thrown
our way: *Oh, love will rock your world. The sweet
sweet fairy tale we spin will certainly beat
the real thing any day. Oh, yes we own
you now. We sang you pliable and clue-
less, waiting, waiting, oh the dream you'll hug
one day, the boy who craves you right out loud
in front of everyone. But we told you,
we know we did, we preached it with a shrug—
less than perfect love was not allowed.*

Less than perfect love was not allowed.
Temptations begged as if their every sway
depended on you coming home to stay.
Diana whispered air, aloof and proud
to be the perfect girl beneath a shroud
of glitter and a fright she held at bay.
And Michael Jackson, flailing in the fray
of daddy love, succumbed to every crowd.
What would we have done if not for them,
wooing us with roses carved of sound
and hiding muck we're born to navigate?
Little did we know that they'd condemn
us to live so tethered to the ground
while every song they sang told us to wait.

Every song they sang told us to wait
and wait we did, our gangly heartbeats stunned
and holding place. Already so outgunned,
we little girls obeyed. And now it's late,
and CDs spinning just intimidate.
The songs all say, *Just look at what you've done,*
you've wished through your whole life. And one by one
your trusting sisters realize they don't rate.
So now, at fifty-plus, I turn around
and see the glitter drifting in my wake
and mingling with the dirt. My dingy dreams
are shoved high on the shelf. They're wrapped and bound
so I can't see and contemplate the ache.
The Temps, all swirl and pivot, conjured schemes.

The Temps, all swirl and pivot, conjured schemes
from soulful throats, relentless booming bass,
then silk where throats should be. Much growling grace
from open window, 'neath the door, pipe dreams—
that soul beneath the vinyl. The Supremes
used to stockpile extra sequins just in case
Diana's Negro hips required more space,
while Smokey penned a lyric dripping cream.
Ask any colored girl, and she will moan,
remembering how love had lied so loud.
I whimpered while the downbeat dangled bait
and taught myself to slow drag, all alone.
Less than perfect love was not allowed
and every song they sang told me to wait.

COLOPHON

Shoulda Been Jimi Savannah was designed at Coffee House Press,
in the historic Grain Belt Brewery's Bottling House
near downtown Minneapolis.
The text is set in Caslon with titles in Protege.

FUNDER ACKNOWLEDGMENT

Coffee House Press is an independent nonprofit literary publisher. Our books are made possible through the generous support of grants and gifts from many foundations, corporate giving programs, state and federal support, and through donations from individuals who believe in the transformational power of literature. Coffee House Press receives major operating support from the Bush Foundation, the Jerome Foundation, the McKnight Foundation, from Target, and in part by a grant provided by the Minnesota State Arts Board, through an appropriation by the Minnesota State Legislature from the Minnesota Arts and Cultural Heritage Fund with money from the vote of the people of Minnesota on November 4, 2008, and a grant from the Wells Fargo Foundation of Minnesota. Coffee House also receives support from: several anonymous donors; Elmer L. and Eleanor J. Andersen Foundation; Suzanne Allen; Around Town Literary Media Guides; Patricia Beithon; Bill Berkson; the James L. and Nancy J. Bildner Foundation; the E. Thomas Binger and Rebecca Rand Fund of the Minneapolis Foundation; the Patrick and Aimee Butler Family Foundation; Ruth and Bruce Dayton; Dorsey & Whitney, LLP; Mary Ebert and Paul Stembler; Fredrikson & Byron, P.A.; Sally French; Jennifer Haugh; Anselm Hollo and Jane Dalrymple-Hollo; Jeffrey Hom; Carl and Heidi Horsch; Stephen and Isabel Keating; the Kenneth Koch Literary Estate; the Lenfestey Family Foundation; Ethan J. Litman; Carol and Aaron Mack; Mary McDermid; Sjur Midness and Briar Andresen; the Rehael Fund of the Minneapolis Foundation; Deborah Reynolds; Schwegman, Lundberg & Woessner, P.A.; John Sjoberg; David Smith; Kiki Smith; Mary Strand and Tom Fraser; Jeffrey Sugerman; Patricia Tilton; the Archie D. & Bertha H. Walker Foundation; Stu Wilson and Mel Barker; the Woessner Freeman Family Foundation; Margaret and Angus Wurtele; and many other generous individual donors.

To you and our many readers across the country,
we send our thanks for your continuing support.

MISSION

The mission of Coffee House Press is to publish exciting, vital, and enduring authors of our time; to delight and inspire readers; to contribute to the cultural life of our community; and to enrich our literary heritage. By building on the best traditions of publishing and the book arts, we produce books that celebrate imagination, innovation in the craft of writing, and the many authentic voices of the American experience.

VISION

LITERATURE. We will promote literature as a vital art form, helping to redefine its role in contemporary life. We will publish authors whose groundbreaking work helps shape the direction of 21st-century literature.

WRITERS. We will foster the careers of our writers by making long-term commitments to their work, allowing them to take risks in form and content.

READERS. Readers of books we publish will experience new perspectives and an expanding intellectual landscape.

PUBLISHING. We will be leaders in developing a sustainable 21st-century model of independent literary publishing, pushing the boundaries of content, form, editing, audience development, and book technologies.

VALUES

Innovation and excellence in all activities

Diversity of people, ideas, and products

Advancing literary knowledge

Community through embracing many cultures

Ethical and highly professional management
and governance practices

Join us in our mission at coffeehousepress.org